DESTROYED FOUNDATIONS

GOD'S CHURCH STRUCTURE AND GOVERNMENT
FIVE-FOLD MINISTRY

BY JOHN DEVRIES

DESTROYED

FOUNDATIONS

*God's Church Structure, Government,
and Five-fold Ministry*

JOHN DEVRIES

*Founder of
Five-Fold Foundation Ministries*

LIBRARY OF CONGRESS CATALOG
CARD NUMBER 96-96552

ISBN (INTERNATIONAL REGISTRY)
NUMBER 0-9652944-0-4

All scriptures from King James Bible

Additonal copies available from:
Five-Fold Foundation Ministries
Box 205
Post Falls ID 83854-0205
United States of America

Printed in the USA by

*M**O**RRIS*
PUBLISHING

3212 E. Hwy 30
Kearney, NE 68847
800-650-7888

ACKNOWLEDGMENTS

The Lord has blessed me with many ministries to encourage me in my ministry and writing of this book. Thank you, Don Fultz; Kevin and Carol Daggitte; Richard and Jo-Anne Blanchard; Keith and Corrie de Vries; Arnie and Cathy Bryan, all of British Columbia Canada. Thank you, Jim McDermot of Lynnwood Wash.; Rick and Bev Nagel of Rathdrum, Idaho; Dixie Sweatman for proofreading; Dorothy Clark of Vision Publishing for typesetting. Thank you *kapatid* apostle Ernesto Balili, of Mindanao, Philippines, and especially my wife (*asawa*) and loyal supporter, Siony. I thank the Lord for those he gives me and all of us to edify and encourage us. Thank you Jesus!

TABLE OF CONTENTS

FORWARD

"Seek ye first the kingdom of God, and His righteousness, and all these things shall be added unto you." Matt. 6:33

The Bible is a very personal book. It is meant to be read by individuals who especially have become concerned about who they are, where they have come from, where they are going. Those who are open to its message will receive the truth, it speaks to the heart. These blessed ones will go on to become examples of what the Word of God can produce. Then we find out the Bible is an instruction book for the family of God. This family becomes His Church, and throughout this growth many of the directives are very clear and unquestionable for every age. This God is the same yesterday, today and forever to the true believer.

The Old Testament is filled with many very identifiable prophecies most of which have already come to pass, like Christ's first coming, His death and resurrection, as well as many other important historic events. Jesus Himself set the pattern for His future Church. This Church is to be based on His five fold plan of ministry - His five foundational pegs to correctly establish His temple, His Church. The Lord is still calling forth some apostles, some prophets, some evangelists and some pastors and teachers according to Ephesians 4:11. Nowhere in the Bible is there even any indication of this pattern being discontinued. In fact, the need is probably greater now than ever before. This message brings out the Lord's plan loud and clear. This apostolic author, like none others I know, has carefully brought this eternal message into the front-line where it belongs. Without this kind of Godly concern in every Christian Church body, the likelihood of Christ finding an assembly "without spot or wrinkle" (Eph. 5:27), would be totally impossible, and we will not see the fulfillment of His plan.

Friends of the Lord, I believe this epistle will truly help you identify where your Church is at in its plan to make a more vital impact in God's kingdom. Yes, you can be identified in that five fold ministry. Yes, you can help others to bring your Church into fulfilling its true Biblical intended goal. Yes, every enemy force can be put to flight when the army of God has its accouterments in proper fighting order. Spiritual battles, like others, are won when we are on the offensive. Now is the accepted time to prepare and Go.

Thank you John DeVries, my long time friend and confidant, who after many mission ventures to the Philippines and many other places, has eked out precious time from his work day world, to clearly re-establish this vital message.

Arne Bryan
Founder, Director
Prayer Canada

INTRODUCTION

Millions in the world need to hear the Gospel, and come to salvation. Many millions more have been touched by the gospel, but have never been properly grounded into a proper church structure. Instead of receiving the baby nourishment, help, and comfort that they need, many have died. We bring the babies to the new birth, but often they are left to die.

Although his may not be intentional, it is a reality. One major ministry reports that only one out of ten persons who accepts Christ at an altar call at his crusades gets grounded into a church. Much of this is due to wrong ministry structure and church government. More is due to solo ministries working in God's Kingdom, without being in tandem and flow with the multiple ministry God provided. This applies to the salvation ministry as well as the follow up ministries.

Equally difficult and painful to observe, the great majority of Christians are anemic saints. The majority are not grounded in doctrine, and many could not even guide inquirers through the salvation scriptures to bring them to Christ. We do not have what our Lord and Savior intended for the church, as written in Ephesians 4:11. The church is given apostles, prophets, evangelists, pastors and teachers, for the edification of the body and the maturing of the saints.

Our Lord gave apostles and all the other ministries mentioned in the New Testament throughout the entire church age. Mankind and the devil have stolen and torn this structure, crippling the true potential of church growth. God is restoring his church before the great and notable day of the Lord! May we all see and take our place in his end time army. May the church rise up and be a mighty power in these last days. May the violent take the kingdom by force. May we not accept less than God has for us in this day. How will this be? It is not by might, and not by power, but by my Spirit, says the Lord.

ix

"For Zion's sake will I not hold my peace, and for Jerusalem's sake I will not rest, until the righteousness thereof go forth as brightness, and the salvation thereof as a lamp that burneth. And the Gentiles shall see thy righteousness, and all kings thy glory" (Isai. 62:1).

God is restoring the church with multiple ministry eldership, including apostles, prophets, teachers, evangelists and pastors. This will incorporate other elders and deacons, helps, gifts, and governments. All of this *today*!

THE CHURCH

THE CHURCH OF GOD, I CAN NOT PEN,
THE VALUE OF THAT HOLY GEM,
THAT FILLS THAT GLORIOUS DIADEM,
THAT GRACES OUR IMMANUEL'S HEAD,
MADE OF SAINTS RISEN, FROM THE DEAD,
  PREDESTINATED TO BE WED,

OH GLORY! EARTH'S IMPOVERISHED WORD,
FOREVER TO BE WITH OUR LORD,
RESTORED, THROUGH FIRE AND DEATH AND
SWORD,
BEYOND EARTH'S TOILS AND SUFFERING
PAIN,
  A THRONE WITH JESUS, OURS TO GAIN,

OH BLESSED THOUGHT, MY WORDS DO FAIL,
COMPARED TO THAT ALL VISIONS PALE,
AND ALL WITHIN ME CRIES, ALL HAIL!
AND PRAISE BE TO THAT HOLY ONE,
MY SAVIOR CHRIST, GOD'S ONLY SON,
  WHO BY HIS MIGHT OUR BATTLE WON!

REDEEMED TO BE HIS VERY OWN,
PRESENTED SPOTLESS AT GOD'S THRONE,
OH GLORIOUS MYSTERY, HEAVENLY
THOUGHT,
DIVINE REDEMPTION HE HAS WROUGHT,
ETERNAL LIFE, AND SINS FORGIVEN,
  NEW HEAVENS AND EARTH, FOREVER
LIVING,

BEYOND THE REACH OF SIN AND DEATH,
WITH JESUS OUR MAJESTIC HEAD,
WE'LL KNEEL AND WORSHIP AT HIS

THRONE,
ONE WITH OUR GOD, HIS VERY OWN.
ALL OTHER THINGS AND THOUGHTS
THOUGH RARE,
    NOTHING I KNOW, COULD ERE COMPARE!

Chapter 1

DEAR CHARLIE

Dear Charlie,

I'm long overdue in writing you a letter, but I do think of you and your family from time to time, as the Lord lays you on my heart, and I remember you and yours in prayer. I always think of you as a special brother. There is so much that I want to share with you, I hardly know where to start. Siony and I were watching the news the other day, and the topic was a small U.S.A. midwest town. They had enacted a law that held the parents responsible to the point of putting them in jail, for misdemeanors of their children. A single mom had been given a jail sentence, because her underage son had been caught smoking, and there were more cases like that. The distraught mom was being interviewed on camera and said, "I discipline my son as much as I can at home, but I cannot watch him twenty-four hours a day. This is so unfair."

On a different channel at another time, two equally distraught parents declared their sorrow over having their children removed from their home, under the heading of child abuse, because they disciplined them by spanking. On the one hand, limits were set in an ungodly fashion, and on the other hand folks were held accountable while their hands are tied.

As I was sitting there, semi-numb with the unfolding of these incredible events, the Lord reminded me of the scripture in Psalm 11:3, where the writer said, "If the foundations be destroyed, what shall the righteous do?" I understood what the Holy Spirit was saying, and thought of how another writer had said, "He who forsakes his God, forsakes his own mercy." In many ways, the western nations have forsaken their God and thereby their own mercy. The foundations of our society are being destroyed, righteous judgment falls by the wayside, and we forsake our only mercy.

How could this happen to the North American continent, where the currency of one of the nations says "In God we trust"? I believe it is because we no longer uphold the principles these nations were built on. These nations were built on the principles of Godliness. The founding fathers in Canada and the United States of America believed in the scripture that says, "Righteousness exalts a nation." Our forefathers incorporated Godly principals into the foundations on which Canada and the U.S.A. were built. In these days the fabric of our societies is eroding, and this erosion begins with the forsaking of our God. When I really think about this, it tears my heart, Charlie, and I know it grieves the heart of God so much more.

As I was pondering how immense this situation really is, my thoughts turned to the church of Jesus Christ, and how those who under God are to uphold a standard of righteousness and be the salt of the earth and a light to these nations and the world. With a deep sadness I realize that one reason we are not achieving all that we were intended to achieve is that Psalm 11:3 also applies to the church at large. The damage is very real, yet few see it. Some of the foundation is destroyed, but the Chief corner stone (Eph. 2:20) is still on the throne. We do praise God for the existing church, even if it lacks understanding. The virtue it has is by His grace. I thank the Lord for every child of God redeemed by the blood, and those who are partakers of the everlasting covenant of His grace.

From the time I got saved, as you well know, my life has been a bumpy road. It has been difficult to find a level playing field. Much of this is because I always ask questions, and some folks take exception to that. Much more is because I keep dealing with life's issues, focused from a pivot point of scriptural guidelines, and that challenging the status quo. From the time I was a young Christian and until now, I have had many mind stressing questions on a number of topics. Sad to say, most of my questions fell on deaf ears. Unfortunately, my ears have also been deaf to some of your questions, while you have been struggling for understanding and answers. They will not be in the future. Please

14

forgive me, and I ask the Lord to help me forgive others. By this writing, I want to set some of the record straight.

Over the years, some of my questions were:
- Am I called of God to a ministry, and if so, what is that ministry?
- What is the call of God?
- Do I need to complete a course of studies in Bible school to enter the call of God?
- Why did that mature ministry not see my heart, and leave me with a heart-ache, and in a vacuum?
- Why the lack of understanding? Why did that ministry not understand my heart, and not seem to care?
- How is the church supposed to operate anyhow?
- How do I flow and fit in with the ministry of the church?
- More than that, how do I make my life effective for God and eternity?
- I want to minister, and be effective for God, but how can things work financially?
- How and where do I begin with ministry?
- What is my ministry, and did I hear the voice of God?
- I know of a divorced ministry, who I believe is innocent, who now carries a church stigma. Somehow this does not seem right. Is there no proper judgment in the church? I believe in the workings and gifts of the Holy Spirit, but why are things not like what I read about in the New Testament, *especially the book of Acts?*

I have wanted to write you a letter about some of these topics for some time. So much of this is so very important, especially ministry as to the call of God. Perhaps I should have communicated with you a long time ago. I sincerely apologize for the tardiness, but it has been a long struggle to get a clear picture of what I want to share. I do ask you to carefully read and weigh what I want to communicate in the following pages.

As you know, Charlie, the Lord has allowed me to experience a lot of things, including street and teen ministry, pastoral ministry, overseas crusades, church planting, and seminars. All of these things were important, but not nearly as important as what I want to share with you now. Please take the time to review any and all scriptural references that I refer to. They will really tell my story and beliefs so much better than I ever will. You know I respect you, and we both know each other well enough to appreciate that neither of us is interested in the mere opinions of man. We want only those thoughts that can be upheld by the word of God. Thank you so much, for your time, patience, genuine interest ,and trust in me, that you want to hear me out. I believe that you are a Berean at heart or I would not have written to you (Acts 17:10 and 11). May we search the scriptures daily, to see if these things be so. I love you as a brother, always desiring God's very best for you. Please keep me in your prayers.

As you well know, all of us have experiences in life which are as diverse as our backgrounds. My beginnings were in a humble European immigrant family. They were clean, honest, hard working, and forthright folk, who migrated from post war Holland to eastern Canada in the early fifties. As far back as I can remember, Mom always got us spruced up, with hair combed, shoes shined, and Sunday best clothes, to attend church on Sundays. Mom or Dad always read to me, and the rest of the nine children before me, bed time stories out of the native tongue, children's Bible story book. I remember attending Sunday school and catechism. At the appropriate age of 16, along with a group of equally nervous young people, I expressed my faith before the entire church. I stated my belief that the Bible was the word of God, and that this particular Calvinistic church was the closest thing to the correct and perfect church. I had never visited any other. This was done without hypocrisy, as I always believed in God and the Bible. I might have been somewhat prejudiced, but I truly believed that the church in which I was raised was the only real church, as all other churches had things wrong with them.

At the ripe age of eighteen, I left home for the big city, Toronto, Ontario. I began a business career which involved travel, and eventually I was transferred to the west coast. In the suburbs of Vancouver B.C., at the age of twenty-two, life took on a whole new meaning. I was no longer influenced by my older brother Keith, who had faithfully kept half an eye on me in Toronto, and felt a new freedom from outer constraints. This included drifting away from regular church attendance.

The next three years I concentrated heavily on business affairs, and at the end of it all, I received an education in betrayal by the upper echelons of a corporate structure. My background had not prepared me for this; I was blessed with an absence of experience in betrayal. Hurt and angry, I resigned, turned in my company car and expense account, and spent the next six months nursing my wounds. This included shooting pool, playing poker, trout fishing, smoking some pot, and spending a minor amount of time with my small family. On one early spring "fishing trip" with three friends, on which we never intended to get our lines wet, I found myself sitting high up on a mountain side overlooking Ross Lake, in B.C., Canada.

There I was, at the age of twenty-five, disillusioned with life, struggling with the decision of where to go from there, as all roads up until that time had led nowhere. I was sitting on a rock, in a place of seclusion, away from my friends, thinking about life. There, ten feet below the thaw line, I observed the miracle of tiny bright blue flowers growing at my feet and was stricken with awe. When I saw a few of them, my eyes would focus and see hundreds of them. The place I was sitting was probably covered with snow just a week before. Wow! Those little blue flowers drew my thoughts toward creation and God. I picked one of the tiny fellows, and slowly picked it apart, petal by petal. Then with my face turned towards heaven, I reached out to God in the unspoken words of my heart, and said, "God, surely there has to be more to life than what I have experienced. If you will just let me know that you see me and know my thoughts, I will try to search you out, and understand what you are all about." That was the beginning, Charlie. My life has never been the same since.

Something happened, although it is difficult to explain. A real peace entered my heart and stilled a hundred questions. Things got so quiet, it was scary. Within minutes I wanted to go home, and see my little family, which I regretted neglecting. When I informed my buddies I intended to head out, Ken Harvie said, "I am coming with you." We left the other two behind, befuddled at our early departure. As we were driving down the Fraser valley, Ken turned to me and asked, "What happened to you?" I had not said a word, but somehow he had noticed. I tried to explain to him, and that big tough guy broke into violent tears, and loudly said, "I know it's true, I know it's true." I had never noticed the slightest trace of religion in his entire makeup.

The most profound by-product of this happening made my wife and brother-in-law stare at me and question my sanity. I picked up my Bible day after day. The nightly routine at our home was to turn on the TV at eight o'clock, watch a duster (cowboy movie), then head off to bed. From that day on, I would watch the movie, shake hands with my wife and say good night, hunker down in my lazy chair, and read my Bible until midnight or later night after night. While reading one of those late evenings, I became aware of the significance of faith. Faith not only in the existence of God, but a defenses down, no fear of judgment, our *Father* in heaven type of faith. Later I read where James says, so you believe in God, so what? Devils do and tremble (Jms. 2:19). I also learned the values of Hebrews 11:6, where the writer explains we must believe that God exists, and that He promises to be the rewarder of those who diligently seek Him.

My faith had changed. I had a new faith and trust in God's love, forgiveness, and goodness towards me! The same kind of faith Abraham had. Faith, not only in God's existence, the Bible, creation, heaven and hell, but His acceptance of my person, His forgiveness of my sins, His mercy and love for me. I no longer felt I had to serve God for fear of going to hell if I didn't, but because I wanted to. God had shown me His heart. He loved me and I knew it. In that so hard to describe moment on that mountain side, He had let me know that He knew where I was, and therefore knew all about me.

Romans chapter four confirmed to me that heaven and eternal life were mine, and I was filled with the joy and glory of that thought. There I was, at one o'clock in the morning, wishing that I could share all of this with somebody. The Creator who had made that little blue flower and me, had touched my life, and now I knew there was a purpose. Awesome. I wondered if anyone I knew would understand. I would not have understood, had someone tried to share this joy with me before those recent events.

Then, in a moment of time, my joy turned into a deep fear and horror. I realized that had I not come to that mountain side experience, I would have missed God and be headed for a lost eternity. I knew for sure, that even though I had been baptized as an infant and had a religious background, I would have been lost. This made me think of my family, and wonder how many more there were like myself, hoping they were okay with God, having a faith in His existence and history, when in fact they were not okay, and had no saving faith.

Today I know the scriptures better and know that Revelation 21:8 says, "But the fearful and unbelieving shall have their part in the lake of fire." I know that describes my case. I was fearful of meeting God, and had no saving faith. Charlie, this started me on the road to searching and studying the Bible for answers. I also studied the church teachings and doctrines, which I had been exposed to all of my early life, and at the end of it all, I have come to some really sad conclusions. But for the grace of God, the item that almost cost me my salvation was bad doctrine and Bible understanding. This point is much larger than I initially thought. I pray that the Lord will help me to communicate to you clearly the importance of that statement, and all that is weighing on my heart in regard to it. The truths I want to share with you will affect your life as well, Charlie, and because of the ignorance we have labored under, we all have suffered so much unnecessary pain. You, I, and the entire body of Christ.

Chapter 2

THE THIEF
& STOLEN DOCTRINES

The Thief

The thief comes to kill, steal, and destroy (John 10:10). How terribly true that statement is, and the damage done is immeasurable.

The first stolen doctrine of several I wish to focus on is the **New Birth.** By and large, this doctrine was almost non-existent for fifteen hundred years. As an average religious heathen, I grew up thinking I might make it into heaven, and would not know for sure, guaranteed sure, until I died. My parents and peers, as good as they were, never knew any better. They thought the phrase *born again* was a Baptist cliché that Billy Graham had mentioned once or twice. My parents respected Billy Graham, but he was a Baptist, and that was part of Baptist teachings. Along with many others, I had never heard this text presented as a must in the church we grew up in. How many souls have attended various churches over the ages, but have been lost because they were not made aware of this truth.

John 3:1 to 3 begins with the account of a well meaning, searching Jewish leader, Nicodemus. He was told by the Lord Jesus Christ himself that unless a man is born again, he could not see the kingdom of God, let alone enter the kingdom of God (verse 5). Since Jesus Christ, the Lord of all, God manifested in the flesh, the child that was born for us, who is also the Everlasting Father (Isa. 9:6), said, "You cannot enter the Kingdom of God unless you are born again," I suggest we pay attention to that statement. Jesus then explains this means a person needs to be born of the Spirit. In general, the devil has stolen this basic, profound, and fundamental doctrine from the church.

21

Some people in these churches get born again in spite of the lack of teaching. However, multitudes more would if it were taught. Only evangelical and full-gospel churches teach the need for new birth even today. The rest of the churches teach salvation by a variety of unscriptural methods. Usually it is suggested that since their particular church is the closest thing to heaven, and since you are a member, this gives you at least one foot into heaven. How many untold thousands of people, registered as belonging to some church or other, lean on the broken crutch of being infant baptized, or the fact that their parents believe in God. They think these things are worth at least half of the other foot into heaven's gates.

How many more really trust in their good works and keeping the law to save them. Often the law is pointed out to them continually. Many think, "I'm not really that bad." But the scripture says that none are justified by good works and keeping the law (Rom. 3:20). In 1 Corinthians chapter twelve, we are taught that by one Spirit we are baptized into one body. This is one of the several baptisms referred to in Hebrews 6:2. The Holy Spirit does this when we are born again. If we believe every child that is infant baptized is born again, and receives the Spirit of God, we also have to believe and see the evidence of this in the children's lives. We see a number of children, whether Catholic or Protestant, who have no true regard for God. Jesus said to circumcised Jews, "Come unto me." Act out your free will, and express your desire and decision.

Romans 8:9 clearly says, "If any have not the Spirit of Christ, he is none of his." We must have the Holy Spirit within, and be sealed by the Holy Spirit. Ask the vast majority of people if they know for sure that they have the Holy Spirit, and you will get a variety of answers. Most of the time, it will be anything but the right answer, especially if you persist in asking them how they know. I am not saying that there are no born again Christians in these churches. Doubtless there are, and I have been blessed to have met some of them, but they are the exception and not the rule. My parents, now departed to be with the Lord, were exceptions. Most of their children were not born again until their mature years, when they were affected by believers outside their background setting. Today, the majority are born again, and we're praying for the rest.

I will never forget my dad and some of his struggles. After I was saved and 'buried' in baptism, he used to faithfully send me letters, saying, "Son, we are praying for you." Because my decision to get buried (baptized, Rom. 6:4) negated my infant baptism, I was formally excommunicated from that church. One day, at the mature age of eighty, accompanied by Mom, Dad flew across the country to visit me. During that one week visit, the Lord allowed me to pray with him for a miracle. He had a short leg, with problems associated, and it grew out when we prayed. As a result, although he did not understand my theology, he accepted me as a believer. Upon leaving he said, "Son, I enjoyed visiting you, and I know that the Bible never collects dust in your home." We did not debate or even discuss doctrine during the entire visit, only our common relationship with our Savior Jesus Christ.

Only a few months later, he wrote me a heart tearing letter. He communicated how he had received a letter from his aged sister, my aunt in Europe, whom I never met, or was too young to remember. She wrote the following. "All my life I have attended church, and tried to be good, and somehow I know I am close to passing on. Now that the time is near, I need to tell you that I am terrified at the thought of dying, and I do not know what to do. Please brother, help me."

My dad asked me, "Son, how can this be?" It is interesting that he asked me this question, rather than his minister or another older member of the family who attended his church. I only remember answering the question, and I hope the answer was clear. Today that answer would be a lot more focused and direct. I hope, pray, and believe that she received a right understanding before she died. I know our God is gracious.

Millions more are taught by their religious unsaved peers that their state of struggle and unbelief is normal. Over the last four hundred years, there has been a greatly increased focus on John 3:3, "You must be born again." Jesus said that when the blind lead the blind, they shall both fall into a ditch (Math. 15:14). How very, very important, the doctrine of the new birth is, and where it is deleted or omitted, spiritual death occurs. No wonder

Jesus prefaced this statement with "verily verily" (of a truth, of a truth). The only existing state church up until the fifteenth century did not allow any competition, and did not allow the average person to read the Bible. In reality, they still delete this passage from the New Testament, as do many other churches. In the last half century some of their people have been allowed to read the Bible. The devil has robbed the church and people big time. Today, this doctrine is being restored.

In 1991, I ministered at a city wide prayer congress in the capital city of Abra province in the northern Philippines. I had the privilege of being the redress speaker to an honored guest, the third highest government authority of the nation at that time, The Honorable J. Salangas. This gentleman flew in with a number of dignitaries. Many people attended, including a large number of high school students. The Philippines is predominately a Catholic nation, but that is changing. Many are hearing the message of salvation and are challenged to put their faith in the Lord Jesus Christ. Many are repenting from sin and accepting Him as their personal savior, and receiving the baptism of the Holy Spirit.
I knew there was much persecution throughout the nation against the "born again," a label given to evangelicals by the Roman Catholic hierarchy. So in preparation for the occasion, I purchased a Roman Catholic Bible in Manila, the capital of the Philippines.

While I was speaking at the close of the three day prayer congress, I explained that I had acquired a Catholic Bible, and proved this by referring to the additional books which the King James Bible does not have. Then I proceeded to read John 3:3, and preached to them from their Catholic Bible that we must be born again. Due to protocol and the circumstances, there was no room for an altar call, although the challenge to them individually was clear. When I was through speaking, I told the audience that I would leave the Bible on the rostrum, open to the sermon text, for any who desired to examine whether it was an authentic Roman Catholic Bible. I closed in a salvation prayer, and escorted the Honorable J. Salangas to a lunch provided. As I left the hall, several hundred people rushed to see that Bible to make sure this was not some sort of Protestant trick. They, like some of the

Protestant churches, had been taught against this doctrine and God's Word.

We can test the difference between the born again saint, and the religious heathen. This portion of the test consists of honestly assessing which of the following two scenarios we fit into.

1) We take off all the layers of both religious teachings and things we have done, or had done to us, and we look directly into the face of God, eyes shut and in prayer. Then, consider what the Apostle Peter said in 2 Peter 3:13, "We look for new heavens and a new earth, wherein dwelleth righteousness." Are we of those, who aggressively and joyfully look for this? Do we desire a new earth and heavens, and holy righteousness?

2) In Hebrews 10:27, the Bible speaks of those "who are looking for a fearful judgment and fiery indignation." Are we fearful at the thought of facing God?

1 John 3:20-21 says, "If our heart condemn us, God is greater than our heart and knows all things. Beloved, if our heart condemn us not, then we have confidence toward God." Any discomfort associated with reading this text suggests an honest review of your spiritual position is in order. Eternity is at stake.

The Baptism of the Holy Spirit

The second major doctrine that has been stolen from the church, is the Baptism of the Holy Spirit. Talk about robbery by the deceiver of mankind! Sometimes we sing a song that says, "You won't leave here like you came in Jesus name, because the Holy Ghost of Acts is just the same." Many people, including some who are born again, cannot sing that song. There are preachers who cannot sing that song. They have doctrinally changed the Holy Ghost of Acts. They preach a message of unbelief instead of faith. They say that healing, miracles, and the gifts of the Spirit belonged to the early church and the first century. I want to tell you that the Holy Ghost of Acts is still the same!

The church is the church is the church. There is only one true church, made up of all true believers, including first century believers and twentieth century believers (Heb. 12:22-24). The Holy Ghost is **God, the Holy Ghost.** The Holy Ghost in the book of Acts is the same Holy Ghost alive in the church today. He is still the Comforter Jesus promised to send (John 14:16). There are two happenings that John the Baptist and the Lord Jesus Christ taught should experientially happen to every true believer.

• John 3:3-5: We must be born of the Spirit, and then be water baptized.

• John 1:26 & Acts 1:4,5,8 We should be baptized with the Holy Spirit.

We who believe in the holy verbal inspiration of scriptures must consider carefully the exact statement and meaning of what is written, and if our opinions differ with the Word, we change our opinions. Hebrews 6:2 lists six foundation doctrines of the Christian church. The third doctrine is the doctrine of baptisms, plural.

The first baptism is performed by the Holy Spirit (1 Cor. 12:13), when the Holy Spirit baptizes the new believer into the body of Christ at the time they are born again. The second baptism is performed by man when the new believer is immersed in water. The third baptism is performed by the Lord Jesus Christ, when He baptizes the believer with the Holy Ghost (John 1:33). As you read each Bible text about baptism, ask yourself three questions. Who is doing the baptizing? What is one being baptized into? When does this happen? *Baptize* is a totally different word from *born*, and a study of the Greek words which were translated as baptize and born will prove this point.

We need to consider other scriptural points in regard to this. When Jesus was crucified and He cried out "It is finished," the veil in the temple tore in two. That veil always indicated that the way into the presence of God had not yet been made (Heb. 9:8-9). The tearing of the veil from heaven downward at that outcry of the Lord Jesus Christ made an awesome statement from heaven (Heb. 10:19-20). This statement said in giant sign language that the price for sin has now been paid. It said the Holy Spirit can now, in righteousness, dwell in man (1 Cor. 6:19).

When the Lord Jesus rose from the dead and first met His disciples (John 20:22), He breathed on them. Something happened when He did this. At the same time He said, "Receive the Holy Ghost." When the Lord and creator of the universe said

"Receive the Holy Ghost," they received. If you do not accept this, then you believe nothing happened.

I believe something major did happen. They were now born of the Spirit. Their bodies now became the temple of the Holy Ghost (1 Cor. 6:19). The Holy Spirit now witnessed with their spirit that they were children of God (Rom. 8:16). What Jesus said in John 14:17 had come to pass. "You know the Holy Spirit, for He is with you and shall be in you." They were now baptized by the Holy Spirit into one body (1 Cor. 12). Some teach that they in reality did not receive the Spirit at that time, but did later at Pentecost. To consider that is mental foolishness and toying with unbelief of the Holy writ.

Later, these same disciples were told by the Lord Jesus, to wait in Jerusalem (Acts 1:4,5,8). They were to wait for a different experience, spoken of by John the Baptist (John 1:26), and the Lord Jesus in Acts 1:5, concerning the Holy Spirit. "You will be baptized in the Holy Spirit" (not born of), at Pentecost. Tongues and the other eight gifts of the Spirit came with the baptism of the Holy Spirit. They were told that with this empowering, believers would be witnesses unto the ends of the earth. The gospel is still going into the ends of the earth, but we know it has not totally gotten there yet, because then the trumpet would have blown (Math. 24:14). We still need all that the Holy Spirit has for us today.

Peter, explaining the events of Pentecost to an astonished crowd on Pentecost morning, explained that this was the fulfillment of Joel's prophecy in Joel 2:28. He explains that in the last days the Holy Spirit would be poured out on *all* flesh (Acts 2:16-21). If Peter's days were the last days, then our time really qualifies. This "all flesh" means white, brown, black and yellow flesh. This means female flesh and male flesh. Young and elderly flesh. They would prophesy and have visions. Then Peter went on to tell them in verse 38 that if they repented, they would receive and be subject to Joel 2 as well. In Acts 10:44-46 a number of gentiles experienced this even before they were water baptized, and this event was accompanied with experiential tongues. In Acts 11:16 Peter said he was reminded of Jesus' words, that this experience would be called the "baptism of the Holy Spirit" at the occasion of Acts 10:44. He further pointed out in verse 17 that the gentiles received the "like gift." So much for a one time only demonstration to the world, as some say about Acts chapter two.

Born again believers will not receive this experience unless they believe the Word and seek God for it (Luke 11:13 and Acts 8:14-17). Notice how believers who had received the Word needed to submit to the ministry of the body and the laying on of hands to receive this baptism, although the gentiles in Acts 10:44-46 received a sovereign outpouring, evidenced by them speaking in tongues. You can not lock God into a box. In Acts 2:38,39, Peter explained to the crowd the events and outpouring of the Holy Spirit at Pentecost. He told them the promise of the same Holy Spirit was for as many as the Lord would call afar off, unto your children's children, not just the first century. That means you today have the promise of the same experience.

Why is it so difficult for some to believe this is for today? Why do some have it carved in the granite of their minds that the experience had to be changed today? How is it that some have it so firmly established in their thinking that this could not possibly happen in exactly the same way now, and question those who confess that this is precisely what happened to them? Over fifty million Christians in the world today could testify to this experience and the blessings associated. I have never heard a negative report.

In the church I grew up in, folks were told that tongues and those who spoke in tongues were of the devil. Perhaps these presumptuous people could do a teaching on how they came to this conclusion. Perhaps they, in ignorance, were labeling a holy thing of God presumptuously with their blanket assessment. Perhaps these so-called theologians would do well to consider Revelation 21:8, where it says that the fearful and unbelieving will have their part in the lake of fire. Also consider Revelation 22:17, "The Spirit and the bride say come.", This invitation was to the hungry and thirsty, and whosoever will, to take part of the waters of life freely.

This doctrine is the key doctrine that separates the evangelical churches from the full gospel or Pentecostal churches. Many born again Christians think they have it all. Their logic is, that since they have not experienced this, it must be only for some others, or none today. They are leaning on their lack of experience instead of the word of God and His promises to them. Until one believes one will not receive.

The Holy Spirit is a perfect gentleman, and will not proceed beyond our will, invitation, and unbelief. Believers today are impoverished. They are robbed by teachings in unbelief, resulting in anemic saints, void of spiritual experience. Every individual will have to decide personally whether to believe traditional opinions, or the Word of God. Believe, read Luke 11:13 where we are admonished to ask for the Holy Spirit, and seek. It will change your Christian life. To not believe, one would have to take the position that nothing happened to the disciples. The gifts of the Spirit, and all that is taught in 1 Corinthians 12 and 14, come with the baptism of the Holy Spirit. If you believe these chapters were only for the first century church, why not tear them out of your Bible?

I will never forget the profound events of a visit to Alor Sotar, in northern Malaysia in 1986. A Rev. Vance, Crane, sister Steers and I were invited to visit a nearly new charismatic Baptist church work there in the middle of Muslim territory. We did not request it, but the host ministry, with great faith in our ministry gifting, had put up signs stating, "Miracle Crusade. Bring the lame, deaf and dumb." By law, the bottom half of the posters were devoted to the statement "Not for Muslims." Seventy-five percent of the nation is Muslim.

That night we preached to about 200 people. There was an extremely quiet atmosphere in the meeting. Five people responded to an altar call. The fifth person coming forward seemed awkward and insecure, and I had the interpreter ask him, "Why did you come up here?" He did not respond, even when we repeated the question, except to show nervous agitation. We asked the audience if anybody knew this person. From the very back row a man who was obviously Muslim came forward, putting his hands to his mouth and ears, indicating deaf and dumb.

We now understood the quiet atmosphere. With all the faith we could muster, we surrounded this man and prayed over him, realizing that a group of Muslims had read the signs, and purposely hunted up a deaf mute. We also knew that if we did not see an answer to prayer, we would see no more success in reaching Muslims for Christ in that area than our host ministry had experienced. We prayed, and nothing happened. Remembering that Jesus had prayed twice for a blind man on one occasion, we laid hands the man and prayed again, while you could have heard a pin drop. Nothing happened. We prayed earnestly one more time. Nothing happened. In great urgency, we stood there at the front of that church, having all eyes forward, waiting on God prayerfully. At that time, the Lord reminded me of a TV ministry I had observed, Ernest Aingley, who under the same conditions had taken authority over the deaf and dumb spirits. Immediately, I placed my hands over the man's mouth and ears and rebuked the deaf and dumb spirits. The response from the gentleman brought the church to its feet. He snapped his head towards me and made a sound.

The next night the church was loaded with unbelievers and Muslims. The aisles, windows and door openings were jammed with people, and salvation went forth. Praise God for the baptism of the Holy Spirit, and the gifts of the Spirit for today. One miracle often does more in a moment than many other words and actions (Heb. 2:4). Praise God, He is restoring the ministry and gifts of the Holy Spirit, that come with the baptism of the Spirit.

"Now when the apostles which were at Jerusalem heard that Samaria had received the Word of God, they sent unto them Peter and John, who, when they were come down, prayed for them, that they might receive the Holy Ghost: (For as yet He was fallen upon none of them: only they were baptized in the name of the Lord Jesus.) Then laid they (their) hands on them, and they received the Holy Ghost" (Acts 8:14-17).

"And it came to pass, that, while Apollos was at Corinth, Paul having passed through the upper coasts came to Ephesus: and finding certain disciples, he said unto them, 'Have ye received the Holy Ghost since ye believed?" And they said unto him, "We have not so much as heard whether there be any Holy Ghost." And he said unto them, 'Unto what then were ye baptized?' And they said, 'Unto John's baptism.' Then said Paul, 'John verily baptized with the baptism of repentance, saying unto the people, that they should believe on him which

should come after him, that is, on Christ Jesus.' When they heard this, they were baptized in the name of the Lord Jesus. And when Paul had laid his hands upon them, the Holy Ghost came on them; and they spake with tongues, and prophesied. And all the men were about twelve" (Acts 19:1-8).

People do not need to have hands laid on them to be born again. Most of the time, people do need to have hands laid on them by Spirit baptized believers to receive the baptism of the Holy Spirit. There are exceptions to the rule, but the majority of believers receive when hands are laid on them by Spirit baptized believers.

In Acts 8, we find people who had received the Word, were believers, and were baptized, but still needed to submit to the ministry of laying on of hands to receive the baptism of the Holy Spirit. They were only baptized in the name of the Lord Jesus and not the Holy Ghost. In Acts 19, we find disciples years after the crucifixion and tearing of the veil in the temple and after Pentecost, who were obviously born again. They were baptized in the name of the Lord Jesus, but they still did not receive the baptism of the Holy Spirit until hands were laid on them. Even Simon the ex-sorcerer in Acts 8, although he had a wrong spirit, concluded that people received the baptism of the Holy Spirit by the laying on of hands.

Both the doctrine of being born again and the doctrine of the baptism of the Holy Spirit have been virtually deleted from church teachings, except for the last four hundred years. The doctrine of the baptism of the Holy Spirit has only come into a larger acceptance during the last fifty years, and in many places and churches, neither doctrine is taught even today.

Chapter 3

THE CALL OF GOD

God's Call to Ministry

Another great doctrine that has been stolen from the church and which God is restoring in this final hour is what we refer to as *five-fold ministry*. This term refers to the multiple call of God to five distinct, unique, and diversified ministry callings. To understand this term, we need to first clearly understand the different callings of God to the ministry. In my life I have suffered much due to lack of knowledge of these truths. As you thoroughly consider the following, I believe you will conclude this affects you and every believer. We all perish for lack of knowledge.

The call of God is not zeal. The call of God to a five-fold ministry is not being full of the fruit of the Spirit. The call of God is not operating in the gifts of the Spirit. Many of these things may be flowing in one who is called to the ministry, but one may be called of God and be deficient in any or all of these virtues. To prove this with an extreme example, consider that the beloved minister named Demas (Colossians 4:14) had forsaken Paul and probably the ministry, having loved this present world (2 Timothy 4:10).

The identification of the distinct callings in itself may at first glance not seem to be a major issue. As you really come to grips with the topic and gain understanding of the factors involved, it becomes tremendously important. We need to understand the call of God, what it entails, and how to scripturally relate to the distinct callings.

Distinguishing the Callings

We know that Ephesians 4:11 mentions five different ministry callings. It clearly states the Lord Jesus gave apostles, prophets, evangelists, pastors and teachers. We also know 1

Thessalonians 5:12-13, "And we beseech you brethren, *to know them* which labor among you, and are over you in the Lord, and admonish you; and to esteem them very highly in love for their work's sake."

We should know how to identify ministry callings. The call of God can be recognized by two separate things, *burden* and *vision*.

The specific call of God can rarely be identified by gifts of the Spirit, though gifts are part of the package that comes with certain callings and should be functioning as the ministry matures. Gifts of the Spirit are not a test of the call of God, since the Holy Spirit gives several gifts to spirit-baptized believers as he wills (I Cor. 12).

As a young Christian, I wanted to serve God. I had no ambitions to be a "Reverend John" or have any title. The desire to witness, give out gospel tracts, send letters to religious family and so forth never ceased. In the first believing church I attended, the pastor must have seen something in me, because he soon had me teaching Sunday school, leading worship, and serving on the board. A year later I opened a teen center, having a burden in my heart for teens in this small community. I saw them walk by my door daily, and expected that few had salvation. I became active in M-2, a prison ministry founded by Rev. Dick Simmons, who was an inspiration to me. I worked with Full Gospel Business Men, encouraging men toward Christ. At no time did I feel "called of God." I just wanted to serve Him.

A local minister, Rev. Bruce Beckett, asked me to be an assistant pastor and help found a church. While we did this, I completed a ministerial study course, preached, taught the young adults, and was allowed to see a number of evidences of the Lord working through me. I was often asked for a calling card, and I always apologized for not having one. For the first eight years of my Christian life, I did not have a calling card because I did not know what to put on it. I couldn't put "Reverend" or some other ministry title on a card, since I did not believe I was called of God. That was for someone holier than me. If I were called, an angel should visit in the night. The souls I led to salvation, the people I encouraged through Bible school, and the consistent operation of gifts in my life were not enough. These experiences did not add up to being a "called" ministry.

I met people who said they were called of God, but their call was such a mystery and so holy that I did not feel able to question anyone about it. I was sure they had all heard a trumpet blast or at least had a midnight visitation. The topic was holy ground.

One day in 1979 I attended a meeting of a Rev. Ray Bloomfield, a recognized prophet who traveled the world. He prayed over people at the end of his meeting, and since I was struggling with something in my heart, I went forward for prayer. Ray looked at me and said, "You are called of God. You know that, do you not?" That was the last thing I remember until I picked myself up off the floor after being "slain in the Spirit." Because of the power of God on my person, I believed the word and for the first time accepted it in my heart, though I still had many questions.

Later several other people in ministry told me they always knew I was called of God to the ministry. From that time on, I have prayed God would help me understand the call of God. I would pray for people and by the anointing tell them they were called of God. I knew I was right, although I did not fully understand the call, always expecting something more or different.

I made a trip to the Philippines, pouring myself out in ministry for a month. I worked in the Samar Islands region with an apostle named Rizilino Montes. I came home more burdened than ever before with the spiritual need of the region. God began to impart a holy vision to me. He began to paint a picture in my heart and give me a plan of action, a direction to take to deal with the need. I have been working out that plan and vision since then. There have been many heartaches, difficulties, and stumbling blocks on the road to fulfilling the vision, but by God's grace it is still clear and intact today. Hallelujah! Jesus, the author and finisher of our faith, is also the author of the call of God within us (Heb. 12:2; Eph. 4:8). We see the same thing in Scripture. As the prophet Habukkuk was seeking the Lord, the Lord spoke to him and gave him a vision. He was told to write the vision down, and believe and wait for it to be fulfilled (Hab. 2:3).

The call to the ministry is an appointment of Jesus Christ (Eph. 4:8). The evidence of that calling is a work of the Holy Spirit within the individual. The result of that work is a burden of the heart. This burden will be an expression of the heart of Jesus Christ for his church and his people. This burden of the heart will be a driving force from within, motivating the individual to enter the work of the ministry. All efforts to engage in the work of ministry will be a response to the work of the Holy Spirit within.

As you follow the burden, and do what the burden leads you to do, and you continue to follow and do as you are led, the Holy Spirit will impart a vision. That vision will become clearer with time, as you faithfully follow and do what you are led to do at the moment. God can cause the vision to grow. We need to recognize his voice, and not try to build our vision. The difference between man's vision and God's vision is the difference between empire vision and kingdom vision. *Empire vision* is our own ideal for ministry, self governed and selfishly motivated. *Kingdom vision* is a ministry submitted to Christ, with a whole hearted desire to see his Kingdom come, his will be done.

As you begin to listen for the voice and prompting of the Holy Spirit within, and obey those holy nudging, you get direction. It may begin with a burden to share the gospel with a friend who is lost, reach out to a widow or orphan, or dig into the Bible to really understand a topic. If the call of God is on you, there will be a growing desire to share what you have learned. At some point in your walk with God, the Holy Spirit will give a clearer ministry vision. This is not an open vision or the kind promised in Joel 2, but a mind and heart picture to believe for, and a plan to follow.

The difference in callings between ministries is their *burden* and *vision*. Identifying their burden and vision is the key to discerning their call. Observing their gifts helps, but comes after this discernment.

To set this on a scriptural foundation, let's look at Philippians 2:13. "For it is God who works within you, both to *will* and to *do* of his good pleasure." The Lord Jesus calls us and anoints us (Luke 14:26; 2 Tim. 1:11; Acts 9:15; 1 Cor. 1:1). Then the Holy Spirit works within us, teaches us, equips us, and causes us to will and to do of his good pleasure. He grants a holy desire for a holy calling, and works within us a willingness. We want to do this or that. Then he gives us a supernatural endowment of ability to perform the desire. He enables to do the holy desire he has placed within. He never pushes us beyond what we will allow.

"Faithful is he that calleth you, who will also do it" (1 Thessalonians 5:24). Here Paul is telling his spiritual son Timothy a mouthful. He is saying that the faithful God who called him to the ministry will also accomplish the ministry. God will work within him, and through him, to perform this ministry task, as Timothy yields his life and listens and follows.

In Colossians 1:29. Paul says he labored, striving according to his working, who worked in him mightily. He allowed the Lord to place burdens, desires, and directions within him. He followed all these inner workings and did so with all his might. Let's do it, too!

We may be called of God, but if we do our thing, our way, or as others direct, we are following the spirit of man. We may see results due to God's grace, but never as we would by following clear Holy Spirit directions. In my life I have numerous examples demonstrating this truth.

For the first six years I traveled and ministered overseas, I was aggressive and wanted to cram every minute of every day with ministry. I successfully kept very busy, sometimes doing fifty meetings a month. In 1987 I was planning a spring trip, and for some reason I did not have a burning desire or plan for the fourth week. I determined not to fill that week as I could have, unless it was clearly God's direction. A few days later I woke to an overseas collect call from a person I had never met. He had heard I was coming. When I asked the Lord about this request that I hold a crusade in the northern rebel territory, I was hit with a witness of the Spirit or anointing that almost leveled me. It turned out to be the most powerful crusade I had ever held, with the deaf hearing, the dumb speaking, and the lame walking. Today there at least fifty churches and outreaches in that area which began from that Holy Ghost led ministry. Had I not listened to that still, small voice and committed myself to other possibilities, I would have missed that event.

The Spirit of Man

It is difficult to understand the call of God, unless one thoroughly understands the spirit of man. This is discussed somewhat here, and elsewhere in this book. However, the following three texts tell us something powerful, just touching on this topic.

Matthew 22:43 , "He said unto them, How then doth David in spirit call him Lord?"

Luke 1:47, "And my spirit hath rejoiced in God my Savior."

Luke 1:80, "And the child grew, and waxed strong in spirit, and was in the deserts till the day of his showing unto Israel."

Note the small *s* in spirit, denoting the spirit of the individual and not the Spirit of God. 'David in spirit' refers to the prophet David (and king), hearing from God and speaking forth prophetically, as his spirit is joined to, united with, and yielded to the Holy Spirit. Mary said, Lk. 1:46, "my soul doth magnify the Lord, and my spirit has rejoiced." Her spirit man, distinct from her soul man, (mind, will and emotions) rejoiced in the Lord. As the Holy Spirit enlightened her of the profound fact that she would bear the messiah, the illumination of the truth within her spirit man totally lit her up, as she yielded to the Holy Spirit.

John the Baptist grew strong in his spirit man (Math. 2:23, 11:9-15). His spirit man became attuned to the voice and leading of the Holy Spirit. Sin became clear and exceedingly sinful. Holiness became stark and etched in white against a black background. So it is with the call of God. As the Holy Spirit moves upon the spirit of man, he imparts the calling. Look where this work of God took place. Not before a crowd of people, or within the walls of a Bible school, as good as they may be for impartation of truth, but in a weary monotonous desert. John submitted himself to this process, and the result was a holy showing forth. Israel and the world saw a piece of God's handiwork and His craftsmanship from His Holy workshop in the desert. According to the Lord Jesus, John the Baptist was the greatest prophet of all time, perhaps because he was willing to tarry in the wilderness until he was led forth. Consider Habakkuk 2:3, where the called needed to wait and tarry, even in a desert place, by faith. If we do, the vision will surely come to pass.

Note that receiving and walking in the call of God are conditional to our response. That many are called and few are chosen (Math. 22:14) certainly applies to this. Many, like the rich young ruler (Luke 18:18) , will not accept the call of God, not wanting to pay the price. Some will no doubt start on this road in response to the call of God, and perish because they are offended. (Luke 17:1,2) Many more will not know or heed the words of Habakkuk 2:3, where the ministry is told to wait for the God given vision. If they did, and lived by faith, believing the Word of the Lord, the vision would come to pass.

Look at Luke 2: 27, "And he came by the Spirit into the temple." Simeon was led by the Spirit, that is the Holy Spirit, with a capital S. He followed the gentle prompting, as the Holy Spirit pressed on his spirit the desire to go to the temple, and as he followed that leading, he was rewarded with a powerful answer to prayer.

Spirit Man and Conscience

In Romans 2:15, we read, "Which shew the work of the law written in their hearts, their conscience also bearing witness, and their thoughts the mean while accusing or else excusing one another." We find several interesting facts stated here. First, this speaks of the law of God being written on peoples' hearts. We know that the new covenant will include God writing his laws on our hearts (Heb. 9:10,14). Our consciences will be clean because of the shed blood of Christ.

A second observation is that our thoughts can accuse or excuse, and the conscience that bears witness is the referee. The same idea is presented in Hebrews 9:14. We have come to the realization that the blood of Christ has paid the price for our sins and guilt; our conscience is now clean from guilt. The conscience is the spirit of man. The conscience or spirit man can determine guilt or innocence, and is a constant referee on the job. When we are born again, God's Spirit joins to our spirit, and witnesses with our spirit in matters of right and wrong, including whether we belong to him (Rom. 8:16). Also, our spirit man or conscience becomes much more aware of right and wrong.

Consider the Apostle Paul, as we read about him in these scriptures:
Acts 17:16 , "Now while Paul waited for them at Athens, his spirit was stirred in him, when he saw the city wholly given to idolatry."
Acts 18:5, "And when Silas and Timotheus were come from

Macedonia, Paul was pressed in the spirit."

Acts 19:21, "After these things were ended, Paul purposed in the spirit."

Romans 1:9 , "For God is my witness, whom I serve with my spirit in the gospel."

Paul was not saying he was pressed in his heart, mind, or will or that he wanted to preach the Gospel. He was pressed in his spirit (small *s*). The Holy Spirit pressed on his spirit, and his conscience was not seared, as some are so that they are incapable of hearing the voice of Holiness and God (1 Tim. 4:2). He heard well, and the voice on his spirit was so loud that he felt pressed to do the thing that the voice was asking. Paul purposed in his spirit, which means he committed to God to do the thing that he felt led to do by the Holy Spirit. If he disobeyed or varied from that course, he would feel conviction of his conscience, or spirit man, just as he would grieve the Holy Spirit if he did not proceed as directed. Paul served with his spirit, meaning his conscience was sensitive to the direction and prompting of the Holy Spirit seven days a week and twenty four hours a day.

Consider Psalm 42:1,2. "As the hart panteth after the water brooks, so panteth my soul after thee oh God. My soul thirsteth after the living God." David was a prophet, and when the Spirit of God moved on him , he was changed from the natural man. This was demonstrated in his life from time to time. Here we have the soul man, meaning mind, will and emotions, seeking after God. Hunger and desire are the greatest gifts of God. Grant it, Lord, that we may have both today. God can move upon a nation, and impart a holy hunger for the word. God, by the workings of the Holy Spirit, can and does impart holy hunger, conviction of sin, burden, vision, and strength like Samson's (Judges 15:14). See Romans 8:11, "The Spirit shall quicken your mortal body." We can hinder and resist the call of God, or yield to him, surrender our will, and fulfill the call placed upon us. Consider Judas Iscariot, Balaam, Demas who forsook Paul, and others.

"I thank Christ Jesus that he counted me faithful, putting me into the ministry" (1 Tim. 1:12). Small wonder, when you consider how he responded to the voice of the Holy Spirit, or how he allowed his person to be consumed by his burden and vision.

Some examples from Paul's life follow:

• 1 Timothy 1:3. Instructing Timothy to teach doctrine, to preserve the church he loved.

• 1 Timothy 3:1. Setting down leadership qualifications, to defend the church standard and integrity.

• 1 Timothy 6:20 . "Oh Timothy." There is a ton of burden in the "oh." "Keep that which is committed to thy trust." (Don't fail, Timothy my son.)

• Titus 1:4,5. Son Titus, go to Crete and all these other new churches and set leadership in order. There is a lack that will damage the church unless it is addressed.

• Philippians 4:1. "Therefore my dearly beloved brethren, longed for, my joy, and my crown." The spirit of man or the devil never put that burden there.

Eventually Paul simply said, my life is not my own, and it is no longer I that lives but Christ that lives in me. CONSUMED! (Gal. 2:20)

A scripture that demonstrates this point is 1 Corinthians 2:11, where it says the spirit of man knows the things that are in man. In verses 15 and 16, it states that the spiritual man (born of Spirit), judges all things and has the mind of Christ. In Acts 20:22 Paul said that he was bound in the spirit. His spirit man was committed to follow the direction and will of God, and he would sin and grieve his conscience if he did not do that thing.

The call of God includes carrying, within the heart of the called, the burden and weight of the heart of God himself. This is not merely a supernatural gift in operation. There is fire behind the words spoken and the works undertaken. In Jeremiah 9:1, the prophet says, "Oh that my head were waters, and my eyes a fountain of tears, that I could weep for my people." The Spirit of revelation moved on the prophet as he wrote, but the affect on his person was a burden that moved him. It became his burden and caused him to weep. The words were God's, but the emotions and feelings were the prophet's.

Look again at Habakkuk 2:1-3. The prophet had a desire to hear from God, and did four things in preparation for hearing from God. The Lord answered him, telling write the vision down. It is for an appointed time, even if it takes a while, wait for it, it will come to pass. When I first read this I was fascinated by the way the prophet prepared himself to hear from God, and even more that God responded. When God answered, he gave a vision of words and knowledge, not a picture vision. Others could read what was written down. Now this was in chapter two, not chapter one. The man was already a mature prophet and accepted as such, before he received this vision that others could run after. I went to chapter one, verse one to see the beginning of the book, and find enlightenment on the ministry of Habakkuk. I found, "The burden which Habakkuk the prophet did see." He saw and the seeing gave him a burden. "Why dost thou show me iniquity, and cause me to behold grievance?" The burden was from the heart of God, but the man Habakkuk was asked to carry it as a ministry. He struggled as God shared his burden.

Looking at other prophets we see:
- Joel - the word of the Lord
- Amos - the words which he saw
- Obadiah - the vision
- Jonah - the word of the Lord
- Micah - the word of the Lord
- Nahum - the burden (the weight, the contents)
- Habakkuk - the burden
- Zephaniah - the word
- Haggai - the word
- Zechariah - the word
- Malachi - the burden of the word of the Lord

Several prophets point out the burden of the word, not just the word. Likewise today, the truly called ministry will speak of the burden of the word of the Lord, as much as the word given.

Anyone professing to be a ministry, without this burden of the heart, is simply a professional clergyman, regardless of scholastic achievements. Education has simply nothing to do with the call of God. There are many persons today who are not even born again, but still present themselves as representatives of God. They call themselves reverend, priest, bishop, or clergyman. This is no different than what the Lord Jesus had to deal with in his day. At that time they were called Pharisees, and are properly called Pharisees today as well. They are still blind leading the blind into ditches and death (Matt. 15:14, and 23:23-26) Never having experienced the second birth, how can they help others enter the kingdom of God? Just by being what they are, they will gravitate toward teaching a wrong basis of relationship with God.

By God's grace, some will wind up with saving faith under their ministry regardless, since the Word brings life (Phil. 1:15-18). I will never forget holding a gospel crusade on Marapipi Island in the Philippines, off the coast of Samar, with Rizilino Montes in 1982. The island had twenty one *barrios*, or villages, and we were intent on starting a believing church there. On the second day of the crusade, enjoying a move of God with signs following, I attempted to reach out to the person in charge of the only institution there that named the name of Christ. I went to his establishment and personally invited the clergy to be honored guests at that evenings crusade, hoping God would touch them. The invitation was firmly declined. I appealed to them on the common ground of belief, such as the virgin birth and the verbal inspiration of scriptures, to no avail. I was informed that neither point was an absolute, and that they were more into dealing with social programs (Rom. 10:14,15). How can they believe without a preacher?

One dear saint and minister's wife, Mrs. Lavena Allen of Post Falls, Idaho, made the point that if you are happy doing anything else but minister, you are probably not called to the ministry. Conversely, if your heart cries out for the opportunity to be released in ministry, you are probably called. Another consideration on this point is from Proverbs 13:12, "Hope deferred maketh the heart sick: but when the desire cometh, it is a tree of life." Many ministries, called of God, are dysfunctional or not functioning at all, because they don't understand five-fold ministry. Many are weary of fighting for their place. A teacher can become weary of waiting for a pastor to make room for him. There are many called to the ministry who have given up since they are not upheld by their fellow ministries. There is a reality to becoming heart sick when hope is deferred.

Some lord it over God's heritage. They see only their own ministry, which they deify. First Peter 5:2 and 3 says, "Feed the flock of God, neither as being lords over God's heritage." It is sad to say that most ministries ignore Ephesians 4:11. Many others are lorded over and the kingdom of God suffers.

Some are called to the ministry, but their calling is suppressed, due to the cares of work, business, and the fatigue of spiritual warfare. On top of that, they endure the painful rejection of those whose support they need the most, their fellow ministers. Ministries perish due to lack of knowledge by their fellow ministries.

To leave this on a positive note, I encourage you to press on. They that wait upon the Lord shall renew their strength and fly as eagles. The gifts of a man that waits on the Lord will make room for him .

Those who are truly called to the ministry will bow to the lordship of Jesus Christ. They will desire his kingdom, beauty, and grace to become a reality on earth now, and for eternity. They will desire him, and what is his. They should show an attitude of gratitude for what he has done for them personally by substitutionary atonement. Their commitment to ministry should be an outpouring of a grateful heart, and all that they do, give or give up should be an act of worship. Like the awesome example of the apostle John, used of God to write several books of the New Testament, we too should fall at his feet at the realization of who Christ is. We too should be aware that until we do, we are running contrary to his holy person and will. Like the apostle Paul, we too should ask some simple questions.

Paul said, "Who art thou, Lord?" And the Lord said, "I am Jesus whom thou persecutest: it is hard for thee to kick against the pricks." Trembling and astonished, he said, "Lord, what wilt thou have me to do?" (Acts 9:5-6).

The Ministry of Reconciliation

This ministry of reconciliation has been given to all Christians and ministries (2 Cor. 5:19,20). We do not need to be called of God to five-fold ministry to enter into ministry. All ministry is birthed out of a common starting point; it all begins with salvation and our response to God in salvation. Like Paul, we come to the realization that we have been going the wrong way, as a sinner lost without salvation. We see the depth of the chasm and the eternal silence, and all that hell and damnation holds. Then we see the heart of God who created us, and who was betrayed, not only by Adam, but by us personally as well! Look at the Fathers heart, when in perfect unity with the Son and the Holy Ghost, the three in one made a decision. With a love that cannot be measured with mortal minds, and only seen in part, God himself would pay the price for our sin, and in righteousness redeem us. The Father and the Holy Spirit were in Immanuel, God with us, our Savior Christ, in His birth, life, and redemption atonement on Calvary. The exception was that awful moment when he cried out "Why hast thou forsaken me?" so that you and I need never be forsaken. "To wit, that God was in Christ, reconciling the world unto himself, not imputing their trespasses unto them; and hath committed unto us the word of reconciliation." (2 Cor. 5:19).

The ministry of reconciliation involves seeing that there is nothing as important on earth as an unredeemed soul. Even if there is a lack of ability within us to so view humanity, the Holy Spirit illuminates the eyes of our understanding. He makes us see the heart of God himself and his Holy love, without partiality or flaw, for the human race. May we be motivated by the light of that love, to seek out and minister to the lost, weak and weary. If we love him, we will love his, and see and enter into his vision. We will pray, "May thy Kingdom come.... on earth as it is in heaven." We will desire His Holiness, love and peace, now and for eternity. We can not pray this way until we have a holy reverence for the Father and enter into a Holy relationship with him.

Like Jacob of old, we will see a focal point for life and the purpose for the existence of this world. "The scepter shall not depart from Judah, nor a lawgiver from between his feet, until Shiloh come; and unto him shall the gathering of the people be" (Gen. 49:10). We will see the kingship of the lawgiver, and his ultimate appearing as "King of kings, and Lord of lords." We will experience the birth of a vision of the gathering of the people. "And they sang a new song, saying, Thou art worthy to take the book, and to open the seals thereof: for thou wast slain, and hast redeemed us to God by thy blood, out of every kindred, and tongue, and people, and nation" (Rev. 5:9). We will see the goal post, the intent and purpose of the whole thing, and gain a

Kingdom vision. The heart of God himself will be exposed to us, and we will run to accomplish what is in His heart.

Like the disciples before us, we will hear the question, clearly and loudly asked of us, and it will pierce our hearts.

"When they had dined, Jesus saith to Simon Peter, Simon, son of Jonas, lovest thou me more than these? He saith unto him, Yea, Lord; thou knowest that I love thee. He saith unto him, Feed my lambs. He saith to him again the second time, Simon, son of Jonas, lovest thou me? He saith unto him, Yea, Lord; thou knowest that I love thee. He saith unto him, Feed my sheep. He saith unto him the third time, Simon, son of Jonas, lovest thou me? Peter was grieved because he said unto him the third time, Lovest thou me? And he said unto him, Lord, thou knowest all things; thou knowest that I love thee. Jesus saith unto him, Feed my sheep." (Jn. 21:15-17)

We may, in our humanity, spiritual immaturity, and short sighted selfishness have to be asked that question three times as well, before we really respond. The Holy Spirit is gracious, long-suffering, and patient, and will press us into this question again and again, until we say yes Lord, or deny him!

So often we will find it easy to love our redeemer God, and difficult to love our fellow man on the same level. Small wonder that our savior pointed out in Mark 12:30 and 31, "And thou shalt love the Lord thy God with all thy heart, and with all thy soul, and with all thy mind, and with all thy strength: this is the first commandment. And the second is like, namely this, Thou shalt love thy neighbor as thyself." To love your neighbor in righteousness is like unto loving God.

The call of God does not make me a somebody. It makes the Lord Jesus Christ a somebody. It makes Him a King, and me a servant, even though it is an honor above all honors to be his servant. The prophet who Jesus identified as the greatest prophet among men, John the Baptist, once said at the height of his ministry and maturity, "He must increase, but I must decrease" (John 3:30).

The gifts and calling of God are without repentance (Rom. 11:29). Anyone called of God needs to know beyond a shadow of a doubt that the call of God is consistent and for a life time. David, a man after God's heart found this to be true, even after experiencing the bitter taste of failure. He repented and sought the Lord, and went on to fulfill an awesome ministry. We would not have Psalm 51 to encourage us in failure if he had not. The apostle Paul said from his knowledge of God that He who called us into fellowship with his Son is faithful (1 Cor. 1:9). This applies to the call of God to the ministry as well. This is also stated in 2 Tim. 2:12 and 13. "If we suffer, we shall also reign with him: if we deny him, he also will deny us: If we believe not, yet he abideth faithful: he cannot deny himself."

Anyone called of God needs to know Galatians 1:1 and 1:15-16. "Paul, an apostle, (not of men, neither by man, but by Jesus Christ, and God the Father.... But when it pleased God, who separated me from my mother's womb, and called me by his grace, To reveal his Son in me, that I might preach him." We need to know our calling is a holy calling from the Lord himself. We should consider the plan of God for our lives from the foundation of the world. (See 1Tim. 1:12).

Anyone called of God needs to see that his or her responsibility includes the perfecting of the saints, making sure they are grounded and rooted, and protected from every wind of doctrine (Eph. 4:12).

Anyone called of God needs to see the gospel as glorious, and that God counted them as faithful. "According to the glorious gospel of the blessed God, which was committed to my trust. And I thank Christ Jesus our Lord, who hath enabled me, for that he counted me faithful, putting me into the ministry" (1 Tim. 1:11).

Anyone called of God needs to work at and diligently prove their ministry. "But watch thou in all things, endure afflictions, do the work of an evangelist make full proof of thy ministry" (2 Tim. 4:5). Do not simply take the title, but enter into the burden and work of the ministry, as unto our Lord and Savior, and fulfill the vision he will place within your heart.

Chapter 4

FIVE-FOLD MINISTRY

Five Unique Ministry Callings

The church is blessed with five distinct ministry callings. All of them are given to bring the church into maturity, to the measure of Jesus Christ who gave them. "And he gave some, apostles; and some, prophets; and some, evangelists ; and some, pastors and teachers; For the perfecting of the saints, for the work of the ministry, for the edifying of the body of Christ: Till we all come in the unity of the faith, and of the knowledge of the Son of God, unto a perfect man, unto the measure of the stature of the fullness of Christ" (Eph. 4:11-13).

The effect of not understanding the unique and distinct callings can be seen from many vantage points, and some examples follow.

Consider the Godly well meaning graduate Bible school student, who has been successful at bringing some to Christ. His well meaning peers, impressed with the young man's zeal, press him into the pastorate of a small church. As much as he may try to cover this base, he will struggle, if in fact his burden and calling is that of an evangelist. The struggles involved will be immense. The young man will be overburdened in many ways. His true calling has not been discerned, and his ministry will be limited as a result. He will struggle with pastoral visitation, and the load of bearing others' burdens, since he is not equipped the way a called pastor is. Others will probably conclude his struggles are due to his new role, immaturity, and inexperience. The young minister will struggle deeply with a sense of failure, and die a thousand deaths. When he grows into the maturity of his calling, he will not be able to handle pastoral work to a degree . All ministries in maturity should be capable of functioning in the office of another ministry calling to some extent, but never as powerfully as one in maturity called to that specific office. In his immaturity of ministry, the demands placed on this young man may overload him because he is not equipped by the Holy Spirit as he would be in his true calling.

The congregation will struggle as well, since his topic matter will focus on salvation, and our duty to get others saved. Nothing wrong with that topic, but when well saved saints get a perpetual focus on salvation, something goes wrong inside. This needs to be balanced with a pastoral message of comfort, apostolic inspiration, and teachers' doctrine, as well as hearing the heart of God through the prophet. The unbalanced diet will create a host of problems. There may be nothing wrong with the young minister, but the results will be a harvest of wrong in the people. Since his superiors in ignorance placed this expectancy on him, the minister will no doubt compare himself to others, particularly pastors, and he will stamp *failure* on his private score card. He will struggle to get a leadership core together, and not just because of his inexperience.

Consider the difficulty within the heart of one who sits in the pew, called to the ministry, with an elder's heart, but the pastor or other ministry calling in charge does not see him in a proper light.

Consider the loss to the kingdom and church if no one sees a young apostle's heart. They will not strengthen his hands to reach into the territories placed on his heart, and thereby limit evangelization of the world, and this gospel shall go into all the world before the end comes (Math. 24:14).

Why are things not like the book of Acts? Let us consider this. For many years, many of us in the church have bought the lie that miracles are a first century church happening, and ended there. We also accepted the untruth that the baptism of the Holy Spirit was only for that era. The gifts of the Spirit, initially evidenced by the gift of tongues, come with the baptism of the Holy Spirit. Because of the misunderstanding about the baptism and the resulting lack of evidence of gifts which normally accompany this experience, the church concluded that miracles and the gifts of the Spirit were for the early church only, with the odd exception.

This also affected the understanding of multiple callings and ministries. How could you have a prophet unless he operated in the revelation gifts? How could you have an apostle who did not operate in the gift of miracles? We, as Christians, and especially the ministry of God, **must** know and understand, and be able to teach from the scriptures about these things:

• The call of God , and distinctions in callings.
• The specific work and direction of God to the individual.
• Church authority and order, structure and responsibility.
• Scriptural understanding on finances for ministries.
• Judgment in the body of Christ.
• Our attitude and responsibility to and for other ministries.

I believe many things are out of order, and that few people could answer a broad spectrum of questions or teach about the above.

You and I have encountered happenings that brought us heartache. I remember a pastor who was voted out of his church by a majority vote of the church board. Many in the congregation did not agree or understand, and were deeply wounded. Some left, and today still do not attend another church. I remember a young man who married a young lady who attended the same Bible school he did. Within one year, she ran off with another man. This young Godly Bible school student made great effort to win her back, and was willing to forgive, but to no avail. He was clearly the innocent victim of an eventual divorce. He was branded because of this, and was deemed unacceptable for ministry ordination by the church he affiliated with.

A quality church secretary who served God and the church heart and soul, one day woke up to find her husband gone off with another woman. To compound her grief, the ministry and board of her church asked her to resign her position, as she was now a bad example to the world. To the best of my knowledge, she still has not recovered from that double blow. This church was the bad example, and not the woman. A beautiful evangelistic ministry, skilled in music, took the job of church janitor and barely survives, while the pastor ministry of the same church does quite well. That is how things stand at this writing. A mature, Godly church elder completed the two year term to which he was elected, and was displaced by a young business-minded individual. No one saw his tears or his heart. A Godly, anointed ministry was asked to fill out ministerial forms by his affiliate peers, and a question on the form asked, "Do you minister full time, or need to work to support yourself?" When he answered that he did need to work, he was categorized in a demeaning fashion, and affected adversely. A young man with a burden for souls in a far off place, got little or no support to fulfill that burden. No one heard him. Not even the pastor. Surely, there have to be clear and honorable answers for these situations, and many more like them.

Things are out of order because we have not followed the pattern. When Moses was told by God to build the tabernacle, God said, "See that you *make all things according to the pattern* you were shown on the holy mountain" (Ex. 25:40; Heb. 8: 5). God took Moses up mount Sinai, and gave him the ten commandments (Exod. 19). At the same time God gave a detailed description of a tent church structure that he wanted Moses to build, as a special place for God to meet with his people. The construction materials, colors, types of metals, furnishings of the tabernacle, and the specific numbers of things, all portrayed a detailed picture of God and redemption. (Benny Hinn has a terrific video on this topic).

One particular detail that made a specific statement, was a four inch thick woven linen curtain that separated the holy place or sanctuary from the most holy place. The holy place is where the priests ministered before God, and by way of the shed blood of sacrificed animals made atonement for the sins of the people. This typifyed Jesus, the Savior to come. The most holy place behind the curtain or veil could not be entered, because God's presence was there. Man could not enter into the presence of God because sin had not been atoned for (Heb. 9:7,8). The exception was that once a year the high priest, again representing Jesus Christ, our eternal high priest, the lamb of God, went into the most holy place to make atonement for the nation. Praise God! The veil was torn by God Himself when our high priest completed his atonement. (Math. 27:51) The earth quake did not disturb the stones of the temple, but the flexible linen veil was torn from top (heaven) to bottom. The way into God's presence had forever been restored by Messiah's shed blood.

Moses build the temple according to the pattern given him, and the presence of God was there! Today, we have not built according to the pattern. If we would build the tabernacle (church) according to the pattern shown us, we would see a much greater measure of the glory of God! Today we are the church and the temple of the Holy Ghost (1 Cor. 3:16). God has taken us into the heavenly Mount Sion (Heb. 12:22) and shown us the pattern by his Spirit, and detailed it in his holy word. Jesus is Lord, and the living word. He is the Lord of the church, and he said "I will build my church" (Math. 16:18). Today many of us have set about to build *our* church. We have not carefully built the New Testament tabernacle according to the New Testament pattern given us, and in many places the devil has prevailed.

Hear me out and see if this is not so. *We need to repent and get back to the pattern,* and when we do, the glory of God will come down! *Imagine if Moses had not followed instructions and did not install the veil-curtain separating the most holy place. Then God's presence would not have been able to manifest in the tabernacle,* since the priests would die if they attempted to minister there in His presence. He would have destroyed the picture. *Today if we do not carefully search out and follow the New Testament pattern and follow it, we destroy the picture and limit God.* We limit the building of the most precious thing on earth, the church of Jesus Christ.

Five-Fold Ministry

We have followed tradition and the doctrine of men when it comes to our teachings on ordained or called ministers. In Ephesians 4:8, we read that the Lord Jesus, when He ascended up to heaven, after his crucifixion, death and burial, gave gifts unto men, meaning mankind. These were not the gifts of the Spirit as spoken of in 1 Corinthians chapters 12 and 14, which are given to individuals, but *ministries as gifts.* Jesus calls those who are called to do the work of the ministry gifts to mankind. "And He gave some apostles; and some prophets; and some evangelists; and some pastors and teachers" (Eph. 4:11).

The Lord Jesus Christ gave these five ministries to the church for the perfecting of the church (verse 12). That is the **Church**, first century, fifteenth century, and nineteenth century. We are to grow to the stature of Christ! He gave five distinct ministries for this purpose then and now. He is still the Lord of the church and eternal head of the church. He has not changed his plan or his giving. Let us explore this point, in the New Testament.

Traditionally, the church has taught that there were only twelve apostles. When the question of the apostle Paul comes up, people are taught that we do not understand that. Worse yet we are taught that when the eleven apostles who remained after the death of Judas Iscariot choosing Mathias as the replacement apostle, they made a mistake. Eventually God corrected this by identifying Paul. This error in understanding is the root to more error. Correct this error and a whole lot of things come into order. Note that Peter quoted David's prophecy in the Psalms, "Let his days be few; (and) let another take his office (Ps. 69:25, 109:8). Is this an error? God himself would have corrected this entire episode. If you do not believe this you have to guess throughout the Bible as to what was right and wrong. God always points out right from wrong! (choosing Saul as a King)

Let us look at Acts chapters 13 and 14 . Here we find that the Holy Spirit caused Paul and Barnabas to be sent out to do their God-ordained work. If you followed the logic of those who claim that Mathias was a mistake, one might argue that Barnabas should have been the twelfth apostle replacement. Chapter 13:1 it says that they were among prophets and teachers. However, as they proceed on their journey, we find in chapter 14:4 that not only *Paul*, but *Barnabas* as well is called an apostle. While studying this initially, I wondered if that could have been a typing error, but in chapter 14:14, we have a repetition of the same statement, "the apostles Paul and Barnabas." When we add these two apostles to the list given in Acts 1:13 and 26, we now have fourteen apostles. We all accept that there are only twelve original apostles, but the Lord Jesus has never quit giving apostles to the church. Another point of interest is, that *the Jerusalem twelve were acquainted with Barnabas and Paul, and ministered in the same era* (Acts 11:22). We again find this truth verified in 1 Thessalonians chapters 1 and 2. In chapter 1:1 we find that the authors of this book were three persons, Paul, Silvanus, and Timotheus. The repetition of the plural words we, our, us, is consistent through-out the entire book. Chapter 2:6 states, "We might have been burdensome, as the *apostles* of Christ." Note the apostles, plural. Apostle Paul, apostle Silvanus, and apostle Timotheus. Now we have sixteen apostles. A careful study will reveal more as well. The point is that there were and are many more apostles, even today. There are many prophets, teachers, as well as evangelists and pastors, and there have been throughout the entire church age. The Lord Jesus Christ never quit giving all five ministries to the church, and all are needed today for the work of the ministry and the maturing of the saints.

The Lord provided a banquet table for his saints, with a variety of dishes. Each dish is a distinct revelation of his ministry to us. The five-fold ministry is meant to be a revelation of the ministry of Jesus Christ. Consider this:

• Jesus is the apostle. Hebrews 3:1 states, "Wherefore holy brethren, consider the Apostle and high priest of our profession, Jesus Christ."

• Jesus is the prophet. Matthew 13:57 says, "Jesus said unto them, A prophet is not without honor save in his own country." Also see Luke 24:19, "Concerning Jesus of Nazareth, a Prophet mighty in deed."

• Jesus is the teacher. John 3:2 states, "Rabbi we know that you are a teacher come from God, for no man can do these miracles except God be with him." Jesus never refuted this statement.

• Jesus is the Pastor. John 10:11 says, "I am the good Shepherd, I lay my life down for the sheep." See John 10:14 as well.

• Jesus is the evangelist. John 12:32 states, "And I, when I be lifted up (crucified), I will draw all men unto me."

Jesus is the fullness and embodiment of all ministries. All ministries are a reflection of His "Sonshine," although somewhat diluted by immaturity, the flesh and the spirit of man. A ministry called by God and appointed by Jesus images the apostle, prophet, teacher, pastor, or the evangelist ministry of the Lord Jesus Christ. As much as we believe in the scriptures that state "It is no longer I that liveth but Christ that liveth in me," *no man* is the complete revelation of the ministry of Jesus Christ. In Ephesians 4:11, the Bible tells us that Jesus gave some apostles, prophets, evangelists, pastors and teachers. In other words, he gave some apples, oranges, bananas, mangos, and peaches. These are all fruit, but they vary in flavor and composition. He did not give apples, apples and apples, or teachers, teachers, and teachers.

Rather than reading this text with disbelief, let us try to understand, and identify the unique distinguishing characteristics of these callings, or offices. If Ephesians 4:11 concerned tithing or giving, it would have been put under a microscope, preached at least six times a year, and wrung dry of every nuance of thought. Instead it deals with the call of God to the ministry and is hardly ever considered. This text and many more are just simply read over, and most people do not relate to the contents, because they have been obliterated by modern theology. The truths expressed within this text are archived. By virtue of modern teachings, they are no longer considered relevant, and are allocated to a different era, the church then, and not the church now. This should not be.

It is a sad thing that so many people and ministries go through their entire lives serving God in one form of ministry or an other, never having understood their calling. Even more sad, so many ministries do not understand themselves, or are misread and misunderstood by others. Many never reach the maturity and fruitfulness God intended. Many give up, never reaching their intended goal. Many suffer great pain and frustration. We all suffer due to the lack of support by the team ministry God gave but which is not utilized.

To establish the reality of this point, let us consider some scriptures that do not fit in the average church and ministry thinking of today. "Now there were at Antioch, in the church that was there, prophets and teachers, Barnabas, and Symeon that was called Niger, and Lucius of Cyrene, and Manaen the foster brother of Herod the tetrarch, and Saul" (Acts 13:1).

Here we find five ministries flowing together in a spirit of unity, waiting on the Lord. We have five ministries functioning and flowing together, and none of them was a pastor. When Paul and Barnabas left under Holy Ghost direction, the remaining three ministries kept right on flowing. Who preached? Who had the final word? What about financial matters? We ought to find out and make it work.

"And when they were come to Jerusalem, they were received of the church and the apostles and the elders" (Acts 15:4). The leaders were apostles, an office we do not recognize today.

Elders were held in a place of authority, and that place is not properly understood or upheld today in most churches.

"Now in these days there came down prophets from Jerusalem unto Antioch" (Acts 11:27). Here is part of the information that helps us understand the identity of some of those *Jerusalem elders*. These prophets traveled as a ministry team and came to Antioch for a ministry visit. They were recognized as men of God with a calling and deposit of the Lord Jesus Christ within them. They were received and set free to minister. I doubt they even sent a letter of request or notification, since the mail service was elementary, but they were received with joy, and nobody complained about a program being upset. Lord, help us to get back to that. Gracious God, help us by your mercies. May we be what you want us to be. In your church, Lord, be glorified.

Chapter 5

STATE YOUR CALLING

In the beginning of the church, including the earthly ministry of our Lord Jesus Christ, He and all ministries were identified by their particular callings. The Lord Jesus is named an apostle, prophet, teacher, and shepherd in the New Testament church. From Acts to Revelation all ministries
• Knew their callings.
• Identified themselves by their callings.
• Were generally known to others by their callings.

Today we do not seem to have this same understanding or practice. Coming to terms with this will cause us to see just how far we have moved from the New Testament teachings on this subject. Let us look at some of the scriptural support for such a strong statement.

Romans 1:1 says; "Paul, a servant of Jesus Christ, called to be an apostle." This is repeated in the opening verse of 1 Corinthians, 2 Corinthians, Galatians, Ephesians, Colossians, 1 Timothy, 2 Timothy, and Titus.

1 Peter 1:1 and 2:1, says, "Peter, an apostle of Jesus Christ."

Romans. 16:7: "Salute Andronicus and Junia, who are of note among the apostles."

Acts 21:10: "There came from Judea a certain prophet, named Agabus."

Acts 11:27, 29: "And in those days came prophets from Jerusalem, one of them named Agabus."

Acts 13:1: "There were in the church of Antioch, certain prophets, and teachers," such as Barnabas.

Acts 15:32: "Judas and Silas being prophets."

Acts 21:8: "We entered the house of Philip, the evangelist, which was one of the seven."

These callings are also termed offices. They were called to an office, or a specific function. Consider Romans 11:13, "Paul, an apostle, I magnify my *office*." See also Luke 1:8,9, 1 Timothy 3:1,10.

Romans 12:4, "All members have not the same office." This is similar to Eph. 4:11, and holds true today. May we see the scriptural body structure, and not look at the status quo, or what is happening around us. May we embrace the Bible directive, and accept no less.

These ministries knew their callings, or functions. We should today. They identified themselves by stating their office first. Why? Because the people they were addressing knew their function and authority. In the building of a house, we in America need carpenters, plumbers, electricians, painters, and tile setters. These different building trades work together to build the same house.

In the building of the church we were given different ministry trades. When the ministry identified their calling, the people knew their function. Also, the calling is more important than the person. The calling is of Jesus Christ, the architect of the building. The person who is blessed to fulfill the calling, is a servant. Let us honor all ministries for their works sake (1 Tim. 5:17; Rom. 11:13).

There was purpose under the anointing, as to why these ministries identified themselves by their calling. **We today should know and identify ourselves by our callings.**

Consider Paul writing to the Corinthian church. He begins with, "Paul, called to be an apostle of Jesus Christ." Then he continues with his letter. He is saying in humility, "Paul, who is a servant of Jesus Christ, is what I am made to be by the appointment and working of Jesus Christ, my Lord. God's will in my life is for me to be a carpenter, and not an electrician. Or, I am a minister of Jesus Christ, and by his will I am an apostle. Then he takes up this topic again in 1 Corinthians chapter 9:1,2. He expressly focuses on his calling, and proves to them his distinct office. Then, after having made this perfectly clear, in chapter 15:9 he again addresses this topic. After this thorough introduction of his person and calling, in First Corinthians, he begins Second Corinthians with the opening statement, "Paul, an apostle of Jesus Christ, by the will of God."

Either Paul was forgetful that he had made that point, *or* he was proud and boastful of his calling, or there was a Holy Ghost inspired point to this. We conclude there was a point, and rightly so. Consider that he did the same thing in 1 Timothy 1:1, opening with "Paul, an apostle of Jesus Christ," and again focusing on his calling identification in chapter 2:7. Then, having made this crystal clear to Timothy in his first letter, he again opens his second letter with, "Paul, an apostle of Jesus Christ." Timothy was clear as to Paul's calling.

Should there be any doubt left on this point, let us consider 1 Peter 1:1, where Peter also identifies himself with, "Peter, an apostle of Jesus Christ." Again, in 2 Peter 1:1, he begins with, "Simon Peter, a servant and an apostle of Jesus Christ."
I have met many ministries that call themselves pastor or evangelist, who in private divulge that they are apostles, prophets, or teachers. They think the people will not accept them or understand. **Have you ever thought whether God will understand your reluctance to name your calling?** If you believe in five fold ministry, and the reality of Eph. 4:11 for today, why not be bold and line up with the word of God? Stop ministering confusion, and obey the scriptural pattern. Be a servant of God and not of men. State your calling. If you are truly one of the limited number blessed to be called of God to the ministry, wait on the Lord and determine what you are called to be. He will reveal this clearly. He will confirm this through multiple ministry, through your burden and vision, and through the prophetic word. Do not be in haste. Allow the Lord to make your calling clear. Do not guess, but know with a certain knowledge, so that you do not presumptuously sow confusion in the body of Christ.

I have heard some say or write, "You do not need to state your calling, only live it or function in it." This is not correct from several perspectives. First, we are not lining up with the New Testament example, and that alone should change our minds. Second, we are sowing confusion and are not putting faith in the Holy Spirit. He anointed those before us, to specifically identify themselves in their callings. Third, we are saying that our ways are wiser and higher than God's. Fourth, we are not bringing the church to maturity and clarity, since we are not bringing the church into the scriptural pattern. As for me, I want to obey my Lord, and follow His wisdom.

People need to know what to expect from us as ministries, and what our gifting and authority is.

Due to ignorance or immaturity, some do not know what their calling is when first challenged by this theological presentation. Seek the Lord, and surely the same God who changes not, and revealed His distinct callings to those before us, will give us understanding into our calling.

One day someone identified my personal calling prophetically. That made me seek God, to show me and give me understanding. Over the next ten years, I became convinced by many things, including several more "words," some by strangers. As I saw the need to swim upstream, and was challenged and convicted by the Holy Spirit to state my calling, a battle within me began. I knew that I would be misunderstood by some, yet I felt compelled to go against the tide. Now this is the same to me as "I am not ashamed of the gospel of Jesus Christ, it is the power of God unto salvation." May we make the church order, ministry, and structure as clear as our Lord wants us to. If it is according to the word, let us do it.

Chapter 6

ELDERSHIP, THE LAYING ON OF HANDS, AND THE SPIRIT OF MAN

Eldership

We need to understand that there is a common denominator to all ministries. All ministries must have the heart of an elder. This is an important topic, and we need to have a closer look at this when we discuss church authority. For now, consider Titus 1:5, "For this cause left I thee in Crete, that thou shouldest set in order the things that are wanting, and ordain elders in every city, as I had appointed thee." *Wanting* means left undone.

WANTING THINGS ! Notice that Titus was not told to find a pastor for every church, as we would do today, and fail to line up with the scriptural pattern. The elders were to be placed to set in order and correct what is lacking. A church without proper leadership is lacking. The elder s—notice the s— were to be placed in plurality to form a plurality leadership. This was to be done in all churches with no exceptions. The elders were to be selected under Titus' authority, and ordained.

Throughout the entire Bible, you will not find a single place where there was no eldership in place,to deal with leadership and ministry matters. Particularly in the New Testament, YOU WILL NOT FIND A SCRIPTURAL EXAMPLE where the church is led by anything other than PLURAL ELDERS.

Yet today you will find variations of leadership that do not compare with the New Testament example. Even in our evangelical and full gospel or Pentecostal churches, you rarely find a leadership structure that compares exactly to the New Testament. There is something wrong with this, and the cost to the church and people of God may be much larger than you may be aware of. When we do not line up with the wisdom and directions set forth for us to follow, we are wise in our own conceits. We are saying that our ways are wiser and higher than Godís ways.

Immediately someone reading this will say, "We have a board or leadership council" or even "elders." We are not interested in the terminology applied to leadership, although that is important for clarity. I am focusing on scriptural eldership.

I challenge every minister, leader, and child of God to search the scriptures and attempt to disprove my statements. The New Testament church was always under eldership. There is more to this topic considering the five-fold ministry; however, let us begin with accepting the fact that every church had an ordained eldership. Look at some scriptures relevant to this topic.

Consider Acts 20:17, "And from Miletus he sent to Ephesus, and called the elders of the church."

Acts 11:29-30, "Then the disciples, every man according to his ability, determined to send relief unto the brethren which dwelt in Judaea: Which also they did, and sent it to the elders by the hands of Barnabas and Saul."

Acts 15:4, "And when they were come to Jerusalem, they were received of the church, and of the apostles and elders, and they declared all things that God had done with them."

From Moses on throughout eternity, and even in heaven to come, there is not a time in which there are not plural plural elders.

Genesis to David, in the Old Testament: Exod. 12:21, "Then Moses called for all the elders of Israel."

Exodus 24:1, "And He said unto Moses, Come up unto the LORD, thou, and Aaron, Nadab, and Abihu, and seventy of the elders of Israel."

David through the prophets: Ezekiel 20:3, "Son of man, speak unto the elders of Israel, and say unto them, Thus saith the Lord GOD; Are ye come to inquire of me?"

Joel 1:14, "Sanctify ye a fast, call a solemn assembly, gather the elders and all the inhabitants of the land into the house of the LORD."

The days of Jesus: Matthew 15:2, "Why do thy disciples transgress the tradition of the elders?"

Matthew 26:59, "Now the chief priests, and elders, and all the council, sought false witness against Jesus, to put Him to death."

In heaven's eternity: Revelation 11:16, "And the four and twenty elders, which sat before God on their seats, fell upon their faces, and worshipped God." According to the words of Jesus himself, twelve of those elders are apostles, yet here are called elders.

Five Fold Ministry and Eldership

What about the five-fold ministry? How do they fit into eldership? The five-fold called ministry are elders, and part of the eldership. Consider Acts 15:4, "And when they were come to Jerusalem, they were received of the church, and of the apostles and elders." Notice that there is a particular naming of authorities, apostles and elders. Peter and John were among the apostles. In 1 Corinthians 12:28, we find an authority order set out, yet we find that they were also elders among elders. See 1 Peter 5:1, "The elders which are among you I exhort, who am also an elder, and a witness of the sufferings of Christ."

3 John 1:1, "The elder unto the well beloved Gaius, whom I love in the truth."

2 John 1:1, "The elder unto the elect lady and her children, whom I love in the truth;."

Also, Philemon 1:9, "Yet for love's sake I rather beseech thee, being such an one as Paul the aged, and now also a prisoner of Jesus Christ. "

In Acts 11:27 we find prophets visiting Antioch from Jerusalem; yet a dozen times we read apostles and elders only in Jerusalem. Therefore this included prophets referred to as elders.

Elders, Bishops, Overseers

There has been much confusion over the correct terminology to identify particular levels of leadership. This is due to a lack of understanding five-fold ministry. We find some calling a senior ministry an overseer or bishop, instead of an apostle or prophet. They are trying to use a scriptural term to identify a ministry placed in a position of responsibility larger than the local church.

The intentions were good, but in error. As you study Acts 20:17 and 28, you will readily see the elders called to meet with Paul are also called overseers in verse 28. Elders oversee, and are therefore called overseers.

Another term is *bishop*. When you read Acts 1:20, observe that the fallen apostle Judas was also called a bishop. Bishop refers to a position, and does not mean all bishops are apostles. We see this by 1 Timothy 3:1, "Iif any man desire the office of a bishop...." *Any man* has the ability to be a bishop. Any man can be an elder if he meets other criteria. The apostle Peter in 1 Peter 5:1 says he also is an elder. He could have said bishop as well (Acts 1:15-20).

In verse 8 of 1 Timothy chapter three, the topic changes to deacons' qualifications. The word elder is not mentioned, although we know the church was under elder authority. The terms elder and bishop can be used interchangeably. Consider the repetitious naming of leadership in thoughout Acts 15. Apostles and elders, with no room for bishop in between, because elders are bishops. In Philippians 1:1 we see two apostles, Paul and Timothy, writing to bishops and deacons. We also know that all churches had ordained elders (Titus 1:5) The bishops were the elders. The authority structure was apostles directing elders and deacons. Finally, in Titus 1 we see that *the same elders in verse five are called bishops in verse seven.*

Are all elders five-fold ministry? No. We find in 1Timothy 3:1, "This is a true saying. If a man desire the office of a bishop, he desireth a good work." Right after bishop / elder qualities are outlined in verse 8, we find deacon qualifications. The text states if *a* man, meaning any man, desires the office of an elder, he desires a good thing. That is totally different than Jesus Christ ascending on high and giving gifts unto mankind (Eph. 4:8). There are therefore two sources of elders, five-fold ministry elders, and any man who desired this office and who is properly ordained to eldership.

Ordination was a specific dealing, and involved the laying on of hands by the senior ministry of Titus (Titus 1:5).

Ordination

This ORDINATION was a normal spiritual event, through-out the entire new testament. This should be the normal procedure today. It should not become a religious exercise with empty hands laid on empty heads. It is a spiritual event, where there is an impartation of the anointing. The laying on of hands should be done by anointed elders, on a prepared and sanctified people, with an understanding of what this really means.

Acts 14:23, "And when they had ordained them elders in every church, and had prayed with fasting, they commended them to the Lord, on whom they believed." This WAS the normal situation in establishing churches of that day, and should be today.

The Laying on of Hands

This doctrine is a very important topic, and listed among the six foundation doctrines in Hebrews 6:2. "...the doctrine of baptisms, and of laying on of hands, and of resurrection of the dead, and of eternal judgment." This is a doctrine that deals with the ministry of the body of Christ, and to people other than believers.
Mark 6:5,"And He could there do no mighty work, save that He laid His hands upon a few sick folk, and healed them."

We see that the laying on of hands is for an impartation. Impartation means that Almighty God sets anointed ministries in place, honors them, and blesses their hands in ministry. When all of His principles are met, He allows them to be a conduit for impartation of His Holy anointing and gifting. This is why we read about the Lord working with them, confirming the word with signs following (Mark 16:20).
Usually this impartation is done through the ministry of laying on of hands. We find Paul speaking of this in Romans 1:11, "For I long to see you, that I may impart unto you some spiritual gift, to the end that you may be established."

In my ministry I have seen this a number of times. I particularly recall a young woman from India attending Bible school at

Alor Sotar in Malaysia. As I was ministering to a class of students with the laying on of hands, I saw a powerful move of God. I would pray for a student, give him or her a short word, and he or she would be slain in the Spirit. As I ministered to this one particular student, the Lord gave me the word for her, "As of this moment you will pray for the things that I pray for and see results." I left that class when the Lord revealed I was to go, with many slain in the Spirit. As I was walking down a long corridor in the building, the pastor ran up behind me and told me how the students had mobbed this young lady when I left the room. They were being touched by God and healed.

Even a questionable person such as Simon the ex-sorcerer realized that the Holy Ghost was imparted by the ministry of laying on of hands. He offered money to attempt to purchase this ministry power, and was soundly rebuked by Peter (Acts 8:18).

Timothy received an impartation of a spiritual gift when Paul laid his hands on him and ministered to him (1 Tim. 4:14). "Neglect not the gift that is in the which was given thee by prophecy, and the laying on of hands, of the presbytery."
We see this practiced in the ordination of the first seven deacons (Acts 6:6). "The deacons were set before the apostles, and when they had prayed they laid their hands on them."

Acts 13:3, "And when they had fasted and prayed, and laid their hands on them, they sent them away."

Acts 19:6, "And when Paul had laid his hands upon them, the Holy Ghost came on them, and they spoke with tongues and prophesied." The Holy Spirit knows and follows the intent of the situation. When hands are laid on people for healing, they will be healed, and when hands are laid on people for an impartation, they receive the gift (1 Tim. 4:14). In any case, the impartation is given for a life time.

Romans 11:29, "For the gifts and calling of God are without repentance." This means the impartation is meant for a functional equipping of the individual for his / her life time of service to God. This means that an elders walk is a lifelong walk. The person is not to be voted in or out.

We should hear their hearts, and prayfully consider what they feel God is leading them to do. Deal with each other before

God, the judge of all the earth, in integrity, esteeming each other better than self. (Phil. 2:3). "Let nothing be done through strife or vainglory; but in lowliness of mind let each esteem other better than themselves."

The Spirit of Man

The soul realm and the spirit of man can be a real problem to the ministry, since we are vulnerable to looking for the soulish approval of man more than the approval of God. The spirit of man is his conscience, which governs what the mind and soul will do by allowing or convicting of sin and wrong. When the spirit of man is lacking sensitivity due to soulish desire overriding that small still voice, we have spiritual problems. The Bible tells us some people have their consciences seared as with a hot iron, and are incapable of hearing and discerning right and wrong (1 Tim. 4:2).

Let us look at the spirit of man from the scriptures.

1 Thessalonians 5:23 makes a clear distinction between the spirit, soul and body when it says, "May your spirit, soul, and body be preserved unto the coming of the Lord."

Romans 2:15 and 29 really make this point clear. "Which shew the work of the law written in their hearts, their conscience also bearing witness, and their thoughts the mean while accusing or else excusing one another....But he is a Jew, which is one inwardly; and circumcision is that of the heart, in the spirit, and not in the letter; whose praise is not of men, but of God."

We see here that a renewed heart is circumcised spiritually, and the soulish flesh of sin has been cut away. We further see that the spirit of man has also been circumcised, and the conscience or spirit of man is on the job and searching our inner most being, accusing or excusing their every thought. An interesting observation in verse 15 is that the conscience or spirit man actually has the ability to approve or disapprove the thought processes.

1 Corinthians 2:10,11, "The Spirit searches all things, yea the deep things of God. For what man knoweth the things of a man, save the spirit of man which is in him?" Here we find that the Spirit of God, capital S, knows and searches the mind of God, and the spirit of man, small s, knows the things within man.

Proverbs 20:27, "The spirit of man is the candle of the LORD." The spirit of man is the conscience. The inner man, our soul realm, mind, will and emotions, are searched constantly by the conscience, and the conscience is capable of disagreeing with what the mind decides.

An example of this is a believer who looked at his neighbors papaya tree, and observed that a ripe papaya was hanging partially over the property line. He decided in his mind to steal it. His desire for that luscious papaya allowed him to override that small still voice, and he justified himself with the thought that it iwas above his property. He took it into his house and, not having tasted one since last years crop, promptly ate it, enjoying it thoroughly. That night as he went to pray, he was instantly convicted by that inner voice, and had no peace until he yielded to the conviction of the Holy Spirit (John 16:8). His conscience burned and convicted him of sin. In the case of Christians, thier consciences will not drop the matter until it is corrected. This man yielded and committed himself correcting this with his neighbor the next day. Had he not, he would have been instantly convicted again,the moment he turned his heart toward God. Clearly, his mind and conscience were opposed to each other.

There are many New Testament scriptures that deal with the topic of conscience. In Psalm 51:10, David prayed, "Create in me a clean heart, oh God, and renew a right spirit within me" David says it was not simply a matter of the sin of adultery and murder. It was the entire defense system of his being that was faulty. His conscience was overridden by his soulish desires. He allowed himself to get to a place of having a wrong spirit. He allowed himself to get to a place where he ignored the spirit of conviction and his conscience. He saw that his deceit would be exposed, and he went on beyond adultery to murder Uriah. When that right spirit created by God searches my inner being, it will immediately raise up a red flag of danger, when I am in transgression of His holy ways. Who has not failed? May we all pray as David did, "Create a right spirit within me."

We see this point strengthened in Ephesians 4:23 and 24, "And be renewed in the spirit of your mind; And that ye put on the new man, which after God is created in righteousness and true holiness." We see the admonishment to be renewed, not in the mind, but in the spirit of your mind. Your conscience, or spirit man, will be renewed with a holy focus. Paul did just that. "I thank God," he says in 2 Timothy 1:3, "whom I serve from my forefathers with pure conscience."

Paul purposed in spirit, not his mind (Acts 19:21). His spirit man, attuned to the Spirit of God, governed his mind, and would not allow him to vary from his course. We read in Acts 23:1 that he lived before God in good conscience. He further stated in Rom.1:9 that he served God with his spirit, his conscience undefiled.

In Romans 9:1 we hear Paul saying that his conscience bore him witness in the Holy Ghost. Here we see that the Holy Spirit gave an amen, so it is and so be it, to the action and decisions of Paul's spirit man.

Paul admonished the church of Corinth to glorify God in your body and spirit (1 Cor. 6:20). He also points out in Rom. 1:9 that it was God whom he served with his spirit. God was looking for just such a man as Paul, and still looks for such today. The Lord Jesus said so in John 4:24. He told the Samaritan woman that the Father is looking for a people who will worship Him in spirit and truth. Be sure of this fact. You can not worship in truth, unless you worship in spirit. You can not worship in spirit without worshipping in truth. Note the small *s* of spirit, referring to the spirit of man.

Last, we find in 1 Corinthians 8:7 that a person can have a weak conscience. This is due to the fact that they are insecure and lacking sure knowledge. Not being sure of the rights and wrongs of various issues, they are of a weak conscience, never being totally sure whether their actions are right or wrong. Their spirit man is insecure. May we grow in the grace and knowledge of the Lord Jesus Christ, and establish our steps with a certain knowledge and a sure conviction of right.

We need to heed the voice of the Holy Spirit as He speaks to our spirit man, and not simply follow the voice and expectations of man. If we follow man's expectations we will deny the true Lordship of Jesus Christ. We destroy the functioning of the true call of God and His moment by moment direction for us when we do not listen to our spirit man led by the Holy Spirit.

We may be called of God and call Jesus Lord, but in reality we have denied Him the right to give us marching orders. We may know we are commissioned to do a job, but we never inquired about the details of the job. We simply set about to do our own thing. We saw that Ernesto and Kevin were doing this and seemed to be doing all right, so we wanted to be accepted as they were and did what we observed them do. This seemed to be the normal thing to do, and was what my superiors and peers expected of me. We ignored that voice within, or never stopped long enough to hear that voice. We were soldiers who never waited for the voice of the general.

We are all pastors because that is the norm and what is expected of us. People love me and need me, and I am doing what they expect of me. Seeking the approval of man instead of the approval of God. How many ministries once had a bright desire to go to some other nation, but ignored that call and decided to pastor. Lord Jesus, may we pray right now, "Not my will but thine be done." May we have a heart like Paul ,who when he was smitten to the ground, blind and broken, said, "Lord, what wilt thou have me to do?"

All five-fold ministries should have an elder's heart. They should have a heart to feed, protect, and edify the entire church. Because an elder's heart is essential to all the callings, and because they have this heart in common, they can to some degree perform the functions of a ministry other than the one to which they are called. A pastor may give an evangelist's message, but never the way a called evangelist will. An evangelist may attempt to shepherd a flock, but will struggle desperately. His equipping did not truly prepare him for that task, except for his elder's heart. He will struggle and those under him will struggle. A teacher or pastor may start a church, but neither will fulfill the requirements to do this task as an apostle will. A mature teacher will present a Bible truth with a depth that is wonderful. My brother in the flesh is a teacher, God called, and I love to hear him teach. He has an elder's heart, and is recognized as such by many. Yet he is often deprived of functional ministry, due to the fact that he is not a pastor, and would struggle to build a church on his own and apart from a team. The prophet will evangelize, and preach, but will struggle to really pastor a work. None of these situations are a problem, as these people are designed with a Christ centered work in mind, and if they know their calling and will seek out and flow with the other eldership, things will be just fine. We need all of these callings. We need to make room for the other ministry. We need each other. Self sufficiency is a sin! May other elders receive them.

A wonderful evangelist friend of mine went to the northern Philippines with his wife and learned to eat dragonfly soup, in order to eventually lead 100 of this tribe to Christ within a year. After baptizing them, he came home. He begged me to go there and gather them and found a church with structure and leadership, stating, "You have that gift." When I last spoke with him he did not understand five fold ministry, and perhaps I "had that gift" because it fit with my calling.

Let us be clear about one thing. When Paul called for the leadership of the church of Ephesus to meet with him, he called for the elders. He called for a plurality leadership, making no distinctions. Not a pastor and council or board. Then he admonished them, "Take heed therefore unto yourselves, and to all the flock, over the which the Holy Ghost hath made you overseers, to feed the church of God, which He hath purchased with His own blood" (Acts 20:28). *All of the elders were charged with the feeding of the flock.* This means all give word ministry!

All of the elders were made overseers by the Holy Ghost. All of the apostles, prophets, teachers, pastors, and evangelists, as well as any who were ordained because they desired the office of an elder. This is God's normal church. In Acts 13:1, we find a normal situation of teachers, prophets, and apostles (Paul and Barnabas), waiting on the Lord and flowing together.

"And it came to pass when the priests came out of the Most Holy Place (for all the priests who were present had sanctified themselves, without keeping to their divisions), and the Levites who were the singers, all those of Asaph and Heman and Jeduthun, with their sons and their brethren, stood at the east end of the altar, clothed in white linen, having cymbals, stringed instruments and harps, and with them one hundred and twenty priests sounding with trumpets indeed it came to pass, when the trumpeters and singers were AS ONE, to make one sound to be heard in praising and thanking the Lord, and when they lifted up their voice with the trumpets and cymbals and instruments of music, and praised the Lord, saying: For He is good, For His mercy endures forever, that the house, the house of the Lord, was filled with a cloud, so that the priests could not continue ministering because of the cloud; for the glory of the Lord filled

---

Chapter 7

IDENTIFYING CALLINGS

We distinguish the call of God to the five different ministries almost entirely by identifying the burden/vision of the individual. The calling of the ministry is of the Lord Jesus Christ, and the equipping of the ministry is a specific work of the Holy Spirit within. Let us consider the affect of that work, including within you. Let us first deal with the issues that cloud the identification of specific ministries.

First, we must be convinced that the Word of God is specific, that Ephesians 4:11 says exactly what it meant to say, and that it applies today, as the church is still being built (Math. 16:18).

Second, it may be difficult to determine the specific call because a ministry needs to reach a state of development and maturity. Consider Timothy. He was told by Paul to do the work of an evangelist, and prove his ministry. "But watch thou in all things, endure afflictions, do the work of an evangelist, make full proof of thy ministry" (2 Tim. 4:5). If we were observing his ministry progress, we might conclude that he was a fine young evangelist. Unless we had Holy Ghost revelation, we would miss the mark, for in fact, Timothy was called to be an apostle. "Nor of men sought we glory, neither of you, nor of others, when we might have been burdensome, as the apostles of Christ" (1 Thes. 2:6).

Third, and more commonly the problem, in identifying ministries, is the realm of the spirit of man. There are several reasons as to why this is so. Many ministries starting out to serve God will attend a Bible school. Many of these schools encourage and direct all ministries to be pastors; after all, that is all they understand. When those people turn out to be either good, mediocre, or bad pastors, the idea that some of them were not called to be pastors is rarely considered.

This is what I refer to as the realm of the spirit of man. The spirit man has not truly sought out and yielded himself to the Holy Spirit, for His direction, burden and vision, and is all too prone to pleasing and seeking the approval of his fellow man. His conscience has not burned when he read the New Testament and he saw that his circumstances and walk did not line up with what he read. His conscience has not burned when he did not strictly follow that inner voice of the Holy Spirit, and rather followed the directives of man.

Many young ministries see a mature person operating in a particular way, and choose to follow that person as a role model. MANY ROLE MODELS DESIRE THAT THEIR 'TIMOTHYS' BECOME CLONES OF THEMSELVES. They should be encouraging them to become whatever the Lord called them to be. More than this, they should learn to accurately identify their own calling, as well as the calling of the young ministry in training. Many Timothys look at their superior's success in ministry, and man-given accolades, and desire to be approved of men, just as their role model is, rather than seeking the approval of God. This is where the book of Proverbs rings true when the author said "The fear of man brings a snare" (Prov. 29:25).

Let us look at the different callings from the standpoint of a calling in maturity. Such a mature ministry has a holy focus, and is aware of the pit falls of both soulish empire vision and the realm of the spirit of man.

The Pastor

The pastor in maturity is one who has a burden for his people, and the local church. He is constantly on guard, watching who enters in the doors among the flock. He watches for the ones who are not there, being concerned for their safety. His burden is for his local people, and he carries all of them on his heart day and night. Their problems are his problems. His vision is wrapped up in the growth and well being of his local church. Although he may enjoy an occasional invitation outside of his home setting, local or abroad, his vision and burden are for his local church and people. If that burden lifts, he may need to seek God for the reason, or where the Lord is moving him. If the Lord leads him elsewhere, his heart, burden and vision, will be focused on that local work. He belongs in the placement of a shepherd/elder, among the other ministry elders.

The pastor calling is only named once in the New Testament, in Ephesians 4:11. The shepherd of all shepherds said much about this calling. "But when He saw the multitudes, *He was moved with compassion on them*, because they fainted, and were scattered abroad, as sheep having no shepherd: He had compassion on them" (Math. 9:36). A pastor without compassion is a hireling. Every elder should have compassion for the sheep, but especially the pastor. A pastor will see the scattered and want to gather them, comfort them, and protect them. He could also be portrayed as the sheep dog who constantly gathers strays, stands to face anything in protection of the sheep, and would not let a single lamb get lost. In Jesus' day, there was no lack of so-called ministries, such as elders, scribes and Pharisees. As today, there may be many ministries, but few who have the true heart and calling of a shepherd. *They will be more burdened for the wounded, the widow, the lambs and the orphans, and the care of those they have than in church growth.*

"He shall feed His flock like a shepherd: He shall gather the lambs with His arm, and carry them in His bosom, and shall gently lead those that are with young" (Is. 40:11). This text says, "will gather, will carry, will gently lead those with young." What a picture of the true shepherd / pastors heart. This is picturing Jesus our Lord. To a degree this should be said of all elders regardless of callings, if they are truly called of God, but especially the called pastor.

David said in Psalm 23, "The LORD is my shepherd; I shall not want. He maketh me to lie down in green pastures: He leadeth me beside the still waters. He restoreth my soul: He leadeth me in the paths of righteousness for His name's sake." True pastors cause people to feed and lay down in rest. They lead people to security, peace, and quietness, where souls are restored. They never forget the target of leading people into paths of righteousness and Godliness, for His name's sake, knowing His name is merciful and compassionate, long suffering, forgiving iniquity (Exod. 34:6). Pastors must know they are representatives and servants of Him who called them to shepherd.

"I am the good shepherd: the good shepherd giveth His life for the sheep" (Jn. 10:11). A true pastor, as every called ministry, knows that his calling costs him his life. His wife and family must be aware of that aspect of his calling. Some have lost wives who lack understanding, and do not yield to the priority call of God in their husbands' lives. "And every one that hath forsaken houses, or brethren, or sisters, or father, or mother, or *wife*, or children, or lands, for my name's sake, shall receive an hundred fold, and shall inherit everlasting life" (Math. 19:29). "Husbands, love your wives" still applies, but the wife of a ministry should bow to and acknowledge in a spirit of humility the priority call of God upon a ministry's life. May they learn to allow God to have His way in the minister, and not treat that call as "the other woman." Rather, may they honor, love and uphold their spouse as unto the Lord, as he attempts to work out that burden and calling of the Lord upon his, and in some cases her, life.

The Evangelist

The evangelist has a burden for the lost. His parish is both within the church walls and outside the church walls. Within the church, he motivates the body toward evangelism. He has a burden for those headed for hell. His vision is to divert mankind, wherever the Lord leads him, from the road to damnation to the road of salvation. The cry of his heart and his constant message will be, the cross, you are lost without Jesus, the blood was shed for you, there is a day of judgment coming, there is a hell to shun and a heaven to gain, look at the world around you and see the signs of the times. Time is short, make a decision for Jesus.

He has an elder's heart and a concern for the newly saved, although he rarely excels at gathering the new converts, leading them into doctrine, and establishing them. He is capable to a degree of working in the office of a pastor or apostle, but he struggles with establishing leadership. In his heart he would cry out to God, and pray that others would come and take their place of ministry. His desire is to see more people saved. He wants to reach more and more and more, whether it is one person or a thousand. All ministries and Christians should have a desire to see people get saved. All ministries should discern the need of the lost, and function in the office of the evangelist, but only the truly called evangelist has this continuing burning burden and vision.

Many people world-wide know the ministry of Billy Graham. His message is probably one of the best examples of the true evangelist. It has been my privilege to hear him on TV several times over a number of years, and he always preaches a quality evangelistic message. He always focuses on a commitment to Jesus, for the unsaved and back-slider, speaking of the signs of the times and world conditions. He is never associated with the office of a pastor, although, with the heart of an elder, he could probably fill a pastors office for a season. His heart's burden under God would draw him into his calling, as he waits on God's direction.

"And the next day we that were of Paul's company departed, and came unto Caesarea: and we entered into the house of Philip the evangelist, which was one of the seven" (Acts 21:8). In Acts 6:5, we find the selection of the first seven, the deacon ministry. These were men full of the Holy Ghost, who were willing to serve at tables and take oversight of the natural needs of the people. We find that Philip was one of those seven deacons, but as time went by, we are informed that the Lord Jesus called him as a gift to men, and bestowed on him the calling of an evangelist. He was a mighty man of God, and was blessed with a tremendous anointing, casting out demons, healing the sick and performing miracles (Acts 8:6). If an evangelist is baptized in the Holy Spirit, he normally operates in the gifts of healing and miracles as well.

I believe that Stephen, who was also one of those seven deacons, was an evangelist as well, due to the type of ministry he displayed.

We find that Philip preached and converted many to Christ in Samaria, and baptized them. However, the apostles from Jerusalem followed, ministering the baptism of the Holy Spirit to people who already believed and were water baptized, and preaching to the believers, establishing them. We find that after Philip had completed such a giant campaign, he received Holy Ghost direction to search out and minister to only one individual, who had caught God's attention and was searching. God ordered the footsteps of His servant and arranged a divine appointment for a black man who was crying out for understanding, and he found salvation (Acts 8:26). Having baptized the man, Philip jumped into "Elijah's chariot", and was taken supernaturally to Azotus. There we find him seeing the lost and, responding to what was so natural within him, preaching to the world. We find no evidence of him structuring the believers and church, such as we find when the apostles went out, who ordained elders wherever they went (Acts.14:23).

The evangelist is an elder, as all who are called to the ministry are, when they reach a reasonable stage of maturity. *His ministry includes the edifying of the body, and maturing of the saints* (Eph. 4:12). He needs to exercise his unique calling within the body fellowship. It clearly says in Eph. 4 that Jesus gave all five ministries to mature the body. There is a need within the church body, and every believer, that the evangelist is meant to fill. He is divinely equipped to impart whatever that is. Whether we see and understand that is immaterial. God's Holy Word says so, and may we learn to bow to His will. All ministries, and especially pastors, need to repent of their sin of self sufficiency! May we bow to and seek God's pattern for the church, and truly function out of a servant's heart. We must expect and uphold this office within the church as well as outside for Jesus' sake. May we receive from them and seek them out, as precious and appointed of the Lord of all, our savior and redeemer. May we esteem the evangelist as an elder, and give him room in the home church. We should allow him to function as a home ministry, and not just once a year as a revival preacher. He should be honored as a brother and ministry, called by the Lord of the church.

The Teacher

The teacher has a burden in his heart to present the truth. He may at some time be called upon to preach an evangelistic message, but his burden is to minister to and be received by the body. His desire is to establish the believer in sound Bible truths, and part of his heart says, "If the people only knew this, they would not fall into error." His burden is to get into details of scripture instead of overviews of major themes. He wants to present the detail of a major theme. He loathes sloppy usage of scripture. His vision is for the body of Christ, that they may all understand, and be fully taught in all things pertaining to scripture and Godliness. By nature, he prefers to teach a series of teachings, instead of hop, skip and jump inspirational preaching. *His burden and vision is to impart truth, and preserve the saints from error by this impartation of knowledge and understanding.* As a guardian of the flock, he is listening for error. His main burden and vision is for the body, and to build up the believer. Like the pastor, he is a guardian of the flock. His elder's heart focuses on scriptural error. The pastor is much more focused toward the discerning the spirit of the man he is dealing with, what the person walking in the door made of, and listening for weakness, weariness, and defending against potential wolves. The teacher is defensive towards potential untruth, constantly listens for doctrinal beliefs, and constantly weighs the thoughts and beliefs expressed by those he hears. He possesses a great desire to expose scriptural untruth, and correct wrong doctrine.

"Now there were in the church that was at Antioch certain prophets and teachers; as Barnabas, and Simeon that was called Niger, and Lucius of Cyrene, and Manaen, which had been brought up with Herod the tetrarch, and Saul" (Acts 13:1). We find that there were a number of ministries in Antioch, and this included teachers. Barnabas and Paul were not called to be teachers, but were operating in this office. Paul and Barnabas were called to be apostles. "Paul, called to be an apostle of Jesus Christ through the will of God" (1 Cor. 1:1). Why were they referred to as teachers in Acts 13:1? Barnabas was operating as an apostle, and sent out to do the work of an apostle several chapters back.

We find in 1 Timothy 2:7 to 11, that Paul says, "Whereunto I am appointed a preacher, and an apostle, and a teacher of the Gentiles." Also, in 2 Timothy 1:11, "Whereunto I am ordained a preacher, and an apostle, (I speak the truth in Christ, and lie not); a teacher of the Gentiles in faith and verity." We see that Paul is called to be an apostle. He is a preacher, a generalization of ministry callings, but he functions in the office of a teacher. All ministries to a degree function in the office of another calling. We find Paul and Barnabas functioning as such in Antioch, for a time, until the word of the Lord came and said "separate them for the work I have called them to." Apostles flow in other offices more than other ministries.

In any case, there were a number of persons functioning as teachers in Antioch. A pastor had yet to arrive on the scene. Today we seem to think a church can not function without one, yet Antioch did. More than that, they were in a place of walking in Holy Ghost direction with the existing plural eldership. Praise God for our beloved pastors, but the church should function under eldership, including the teacher calling, as well as the pastor, all other callings, and "any man" elders.

The one person commonly accepted as a teacher in the New Testament is Apollos. "And a certain Jew named Apollos, born at Alexandria, an eloquent man, and mighty in the scriptures, came to Ephesus. And when he was disposed to pass into Achaia, the brethren wrote, exhorting the disciples to receive him: who, when he was come, helped them much which had believed through grace: For he mightily convinced the Jews, and that publicly, showing by the scriptures that Jesus was Christ" (Acts 18:2427).

Apollos was mighty in scriptures. He used the sword of the Spirit well, and convinced others by use of the scriptures that the doctrine of the deity of Christ was correct. He focused on setting the record straight when it came to untruth. When others came to him to correct him in his understanding he received it. He desired truth, and was teachable. Acts 18:25 says that he was *fervent in spirit, and he spoke and taught diligently the things of the Lord.* He did not stay in one place consistently, as we see him moving to Corinth in Acts 18:1. He followed apostolic direction, and flowed with the multiple ministry functions. We find that Paul acknowledged Apollos' great value. Paul saw the need for his ministry, and requested him to bless Corinth with his strength.

"As touching our brother Apollos, I greatly desired him to come unto you with the brethren: but his will was not at all to come at this time; but he will come when he shall have convenient time" (1 Cor. 16:12). May the church and all of its ministries receive and identify those elders called to the office of a teacher. This office is distinct from the elder qualification that all elders should be apt to teach (1Tim. 3:1 and 2).

The Prophet

I am blessed to know a number of prophets and prophetesses, but they vary tremendously in ministry focus and personality. Much of what applies to the prophet also applies to the prophetess. They do have several things in common. In particular, *they will reveal and declare the heart of God to men, and expose the heart of men before God* when they minister. This will happen through their preaching as well as the gifts of the Spirit. In 1 Corinthians 14:6 and 26, Paul speaks of some ministering by revelation. This especially applies to the prophet, compared to a teacher who predominantly ministers in doctrine.

Just because someone operates in the gift of prophecy, as taught in 1 Corinthians 12 and 14, does not mean that they are called to the five-fold ministry calling of Ephesians 4:11. Several ministries teach on Bible prophecy today. This does not make them prophets. Most prophets operate in the revelation gifts, and the power gifts of the Spirit in strong measure. Those who focus on teaching Bible prophecy are mostly teachers, or sometimes evangelists.

When we look at the gifts of the Spirit in 1 Corinthians 12 and 14, we see that many and any may receive the gift of prophecy, but the Lord gave some prophets (Eph. 4:11).

1 Corinthians 12:7 to 11, "But the manifestation of the Spirit is given to every man to profit withal. For to one is given by the Spirit the word of wisdom; to another the word of knowledge by the same Spirit; To another faith by the same Spirit; to another the gifts of healing by the same Spirit; To another the working of miracles; to another prophecy; to another discerning of spirits; to another divers kinds of tongues; to another the interpretation of tongues: But all these worketh that selfsame Spirit, dividing to every man severally as He will."

We note that every Spirit-baptized believer receives several gifts of the Spirit, at the Holy Spirit's will and discretion. It is up to us to wait on God, for a release of these gifts, to determine what ours are.

For many years, this awesome foundation ministry of the prophet (Eph. 2:20) seems to have disappeared. Because the doctrine of the new birth was stolen, salvation was limited. Then the doctrine of the baptism of the Holy Spirit, which is only available to the born again child of God, was stolen as well. Believers did not operate in the gifts of the Spirit, since the gifts of the Spirit come with the baptism of the Holy Spirit. How can you receive a prophet, unless he or she functions in the revelation gifts? I am convinced there have been some who in fact functioned in this calling throughout the centuries, even though they were not commonly known or recognized.

The prophet has a unique calling demonstrated in diverse ways. As you consider some of the men described in the Old Testament who fulfilled that calling, you get a glimpse of the extreme differences in personalities. Who would consider that King David(Acts 2:30) had the same calling as Jeremiah, Isaiah, or Jonah? Yet all of them were prophets.

Prophets focus people on an issue that God wants to deal with. They do not always speak that message in prophetic utterance, beginning with "Thus says the Lord," but often carry a specific message in their hearts. They speak forth that message, and focus on that message, much like John The Baptist. It would be difficult to accept a prophet, who in maturity does not operate in the revelation gifts to a degree. This ministry is being restored to the church, mostly in the last century, but it is only in the last few years that we are seeing a larger restoration and acceptance of this ministry.

There have been tremendous prophet and prophetess ministries. Many have been blessed by them, especially in the last fifty years. Consider William Branham in the early fifties. He operated in an awesome way in the gift of the word of knowledge, telling total strangers personal details of their lives, and doing tremendous miracles. I have been blessed by Milfred Kirpatrick, who, when I was a young ministry, pointed me out while I was in the back of a church meeting. He told me what had been going on in my life just previously, and told Dick Edelman, the brother with me, what he had been reading in the Bible for the last week. He also said Dick was called to be a prophet. I was still a stranger to this man when he, by supernatural direction, wound up in a small church I was pastoring, some six hundred miles from where I first saw him. When he ministered there, he affected some of the people in such a way that they have never been the same since, due to an impartation of the revelation gifts. Then later, again by divine appointment, I met him in a home in the City of Manila. This is a city of over ten million people in the Philippines. I was there for two hours, visiting an evangelist, Rev. Rod McDougal, and again it was in the direction of God. Brother Kirpatrick called me by a particular Bible name, never having seen me, or getting to know me.

In a different city, a woman by the name of Mary Goddard also called me by this name and told me several things that came to pass. Again, an American prophet by the name of Johnny Otto, never having met me previously, also called me by the same Bible name. He told me things that came to pass in the following two weeks, on an overseas trip.

One prophet I know, Arne Bryan, heads up a tremendous Prayer ministry across Canada. Arne and his wife Kathy have a burden to see people follow the promises of 2 Chronicles 7:14, "If my people, which are called by my name, shall humble themselves, and pray, and seek my face, and turn from their wicked ways; then will I hear from heaven, and will forgive their sin, and will heal their land." The Lord deals with him through dreams and visions, as well as the occasional prophetic word.

Other prophets I know function continuously in the revelation gifts, sharing what God wants people to know. Their vision is not pastoral, as much as they want to see the hearts of men turned to Christ and holiness. *The prophet ministry is a foundation ministry. In Ephesians 2:20, the apostle Paul says that the church is built on the foundation of apostles and prophets.* This truth tells us something of their burden and vision. The prophet shares with the apostle the desire to see new territory opened and won for Christ. When this is done through evangelism, they continue to carry a burden for that work and ministry. They want to build up that ministry and leadership, focusing people's hearts toward God and the workings of the Holy Spirit. A spirit of travail and intercession will be upon them for that work.

As a rule, when they preach they rarely teach a theological, or in depth doctrinal message, but rather an inspirational message. This is not always the case, as they differ in the ministry of the word. The occasional prophet does focus strongly on doctrine, but he is the exception. One ministry I am blessed by, Johnny

Otto, has a great scriptural memory, and ministers this prophetically, giving people several scriptures that are accurate and Holy Ghost inspired. Another ministry will operate in the gift of the word of knowledge, telling people what has been going on in their lives, and what the Lord wants them to know. Another ministry will have a burning message of what the Lord has on His heart. Some prophets and prophetesses, will travel to a number of nations, and evangelize as well as minister to the body of believers.

I know of a number of women who are prophetesses, and they travel to several nations according to the burden of the Lord on their hearts. It is interesting that they each have a burden and ministry focus toward a certain group of nations, or a particular continent and people. All have a vision and desire to minister and be received by home territory churches. Most will and should work with local eldership and apostles, who will structure the local church, and bond the church works together. Some prophetesses will, on occasion, pastor a work. Due to their calling, they demonstrate an openness to visiting ministries and others functioning in the gifts of the Spirit. If this is their calling, you will see others around them receiving an impartation of the revelation gifts. If they have a clear Kingdom vision, they will seek to flow with five-fold ministry under Christ.

We find the account of Anna, a prophetess at the time of the presentation of the Christ child in Jerusalem (Lk. 2:36). Prophetesses had their place and ministry in the Old Testament as well as the New Testament times. A powerful example of a prophetess who ministered before the Lord and ruled over Israel for twenty years was a woman called Deborah. The Lord put her in a place of judging the nation. More than this, she gave God's direction to the prophets in her day. God will use a woman when He so desires.

When we look at the prophet, consider Genesis 20:7, "Now therefore restore the man his wife; for he is a prophet, and he shall pray for thee." We do not see any prophesying in Abraham's life, yet he had a message and great faith, and was a prophet. He certainly was used of God in a miraculous life of ministry. We do not see him operate in the revelation gifts as we see in the account of Elijah's ministry.

Exodus 7:1, "And the LORD said unto Moses, See, I have made thee a god to Pharaoh: and Aaron thy brother shall be thy prophet." Deuteronomy 34:10, "And there arose not a prophet since in Israel like unto Moses, whom the LORD knew face to face." God made Aaron and Moses prophets.

1 Samuel 3:20, "And all Israel from Dan even to Beersheba knew that Samuel was established to be a prophet of the LORD." Prophets have a visible ministry and as David said, "My heart was hot within me, while I was musing the fire burned: then spake I with my tongue' (Psalm 39:3).

1 Samuel 9:9, "Beforetime in Israel, when a man went to inquire of God, thus he spake, Come, and let us go to the seer: for *he that is now called a Prophet was beforetime called a Seer."* This explains the dual name prophet and seer.

2 Kings 6:12, "And one of his servants said, None, my lord, O king: but Elisha, the prophet that is in Israel, telleth the king of Israel the words that thou speakest in thy bedchamber." Some prophets have this kind of revelation, yet others have a message instead. Jonah and John The Baptist are examples.

Jeremiah 1:5, "Before I formed thee in the belly I knew thee; and before thou camest forth out of the womb I sanctified thee, and I ordained thee a prophet unto the nations." We see here the holy appointment of God.

Jeremiah 6:13, "For from the least of them even unto the greatest of them every one is given to covetousness; and from the prophet even unto the priest every one dealeth falsely." We see here that the call to this ministry does not guarantee perfection.

Daniel 9:2, "In the first year of his reign, I Daniel understood by books the number of the years, whereof the word of the LORD came to Jeremiah the prophet, that He would accomplish seventy years in the desolations of Jerusalem."

Acts 11:28 , "And there stood up one of them named Agabus, and signified by the Spirit that there should be great dearth throughout all the world: which came to pass in the days of Claudius Caesar." Prophets often foretold coming events. The Lord Jesus fulfilled over one hundred specific prophecies that foretold details of His birth, life and death.

1 Corinthians 14:3, "But he that prophesieth speaketh unto men to edification, and exhortation, and comfort," not to con-

demn. Many mistakenly believe this text is fulfilled by exercising anointed preaching. Prophecy is not preaching, but a divine speaking forth by the direction of the Holy Spirit (1 Cor. 12:11), supernatural revelation of the heart of God and His thoughts to an individual. Consider Ezekiel 36:1, where the prophet is told to prophesy to the land of Israel, and foretold by supernatural revelation the scattering and gathering of Israel (verses 18 and 24). True Prophecy enters into the supernatural. The Lord blessed me with a fellow elder, Rick Nagel, who was told a number of things by the Lord, even before he was saved. This prophetic revelation strengthened his person when he needed it most.

I Corinthians 14:24 to 25, "But if all prophesy, and there come in one that believeth not, or one unlearned, he is convinced of all, he is judged of all: And thus are the secrets of his heart made manifest; and so falling down on his face he will worship God, and report that God is in you of a truth." Again, note the supernatural content of prophecy, distinct from Bible word insight. We see here the awesome affect of true prophecy. May the gift increase, and the calling of the prophet be established.

1 Corinthians 14:31, "For ye may all prophesy one by one, that all may learn, and all may be comforted." We are to allow room in our services for prophecy (Acts 4:31).

1 Corinthians 14:32, "And the spirits of the prophets are subject to the prophets." Persons or prophets may act under the anointing, but they are responsible at all times for their actions and behavior. They can never blame odd behavior on the Holy Ghost, as if they personally are not in control. *What ever the Holy Ghost wants them to say needs to be said in the nature of the Holy Ghost*, who is what 1 Corinthians thirteen is all about.

It bothers me and grieves my spirit when a prophet or prophetess prophecies to the assembly of believers in a harsh, shrill spirit. The word may have some revelation truth, but the spirit in which it is delivered destroys both the hearer and the word given.

Ephesians 3:5, "Which in other generations was not made known unto the sons of men, as it hath now been revealed unto His holy apostles and prophets in the Spirit." Prophets receive knowledge about things by the inner supernatural voice of the

Holy Spirit. The revelation of the church is primarily given to apostles and prophets.

Ephesians 3:5b, "As it is now revealed unto His holy apostles and prophets." These texts indicate several things. Prophets are referred to as Holy. We are not to worship prophets, but God alone, yet we are to esteem them for their calling's sake, and thereby in fact reverence Jesus Christ, who called them to a holy calling. These texts also tell us something about the scope of their vision. They see the larger picture or overview of the church, as the Lord speaks to them of gentile nations and the church in its totality. All brethren are called holy and rightly so, and all ministries and people see the teachings of the gospel going to the gentiles, but the revelation came through the prophets and apostles.

Prophets often seem to draw towards each other, travel with, and befriend other prophets. "Now in these days there came down prophets from Jerusalem unto Antioch" (Acts 11:27). Often we find that when they minister in the prophetic revelation gifts, the Spirit of prophecy flows, and moves on different ones, moving from one to the other, and other people and ministries as well.

The Apostle

The apostle, in maturity, has a burden for the church and all believers. This is a burden that extends to the many places he has been. His burden and vision are much larger than the local church. As a mother who has four children carries all of them on her mind, even if for the moment her thoughts are focused on one particular child, likewise an apostle carries all the places that he has been involved with on his mind. Apostles have a vision for the lost and want to break new ground and establish new works. Other ministries may start a gospel work, but not be called to this calling, even though they may, with the heart of an elder, function in this office and fill a present need. The apostle wants to establish and gather new believers together. He will carry them on his heart. He will also carry a number of ministries the Lord will raise up in his life, or that he will be associated with. He is a trail maker, and other ministries will follow those trails. His desire is that any and all churches that he is involved with prosper and be in unity, growing in the Lord, and safe guarded with sound doctrine. He is a guardian of doctrine at all times, and is much involved with teaching and balancing doctrine. We find in Acts 2:42 the people continued steadfastly in the apostles' doctrine, and it specifically said *apostles*.

Often apostles are not accepted or recognized, since most people today have a wrong picture of this ministry, and may not even believe that it exists. They expect a super saint, dressed right, looking spiritual. According to modern and carnal understanding, he must be in "full-time ministry," with an endless experience of mighty anointing, evidenced with miracles. This description definitely should apply on occasion to the apostle, but we may see this calling differently in reality, and more scripturally as well.

In their day, we may have had to visit the local prison to have a talk with John or Paul. It might have been difficult to accept Paul as an apostle, since he apparently backslid more than once. He was found working with his hands, for three whole years on one occasion. He probably had not learned to "live by faith." 2 Thessalonians 3:8 and 9, "Neither did we eat bread for naught at any man's hand, but in labor and travail, working night and day, that we might not burden any of you: not because we have not the right, but to make ourselves and ensample unto you, that ye should imitate us." Perhaps we would not recognize him at all, if we believe his own description of himself. "For, I think, God hath set forth us the apostles last of all, as men doomed to death: for we are made a spectacle unto the world, both to angels and men. We are fools for Christ's sake, but ye are wise in Christ; we are weak, but ye are strong; ye have glory, but we have dishonor. *Even unto this present hour we both hunger, and thirst, and are naked, and are buffeted, and have no certain dwelling-place; and we toil, working with our own hands: being reviled, we bless; being persecuted, we endure; being defamed, we entreat: we are made as the filth of the world, the off scouring of all things, even until now.* I write not these things to shame you, but to admonish you as my beloved children. For though ye have ten thousand tutors in Christ, yet have ye not many fathers" (1 Cor. 4:9-14).

May we recognize the apostle in his calling by his burden and vision.

Apostles and doctrine go together. Other ministries should labor in and contend for sound doctrine and the faith once delivered to the saints, especially the teacher, but the apostle will carry a special burden for sound doctrine. See Paul's focus.

1 Timothy 1:10, "And if there be any other thing contrary to sound doctrine..."

1 Timothy 6:3, "If any man teacheth a different doctrine, and consenteth not to sound words..."

2 Timothy 4:3, "For the time will come when they will not endure sound doctrine."

Titus 1:9, "...holding to the faithful word which is according to the teaching, that he may be able to exhort in sound doctrine."

Titus 2:1, "."But speak thou the things which befit sound doctrine

The apostle lives with the eldership of the various churches he is involved with (Acts 20:28), and remembers them in particular. He always carries a group of 'Timothys' on his heart, particularly if they look to him for direction. Consider Paul's letters to Timothy and Titus.

The apostle has a view of the war effort, spiritually speaking, instead of a battle, much like a five star general. Even if he is doing little, or is simply not recognized, this does not change. Paul's instructions to Titus deal with "every city." When he hears some souls somewhere accepted the gospel, his heart immediately aches for them and he wants to ensure their safety from wolves and error. He wonders if they are all right after coming to birth, and whether someone is taking care of them. He will pray and seek the Lord if this is something the Lord wants him to deal with (Acts 8:14).

The apostle also has a burden for any young ministries that he may encounter; he wants to encourage them and strengthen their vision. Like the prophet, he often identifies them . His desire is to train them, and take them along when they are ready to go to other places. "Now Paul and his company set sail from Paphos" (Acts 13:13).

When things are in order and stable where he is working, his heart (and the Lord) will draw him into new ground to blaze new gospel trails. There he will evangelize, gather the new converts, and spend time introducing young ministries or raising up elders to care for the new group of believers. He derives great joy from seeing other ministries function under his direction. He will love them and carry them on his heart, *not with a spirit of control*, but simply to see them grow and be fruitful. His burden is for the body of Christ.

The apostle has teeth, and will bare them as a guard dog when it comes to protecting the flock from the influence of bad ministries. His vision is to see the gospel go into all the earth, and he will be focused towards a specific area of the world. His desire is to see healthy and balanced churches established there. He will send other ministries to them as the Lord allows to build them up. If he is stationed in a church setting for a time, part of his heart is focused on building up the local body and teaching, but part of his heart will be outside the walls of that established group, thinking of the lost and the other churches. He will rejoice when he hears of gospel advances being made under other ministries anywhere, and elsewhere in the world.

Chapter 8

MINISTRY
AND A RIGHT SPIRIT

We find the statement about the call of God and ministry in Romans 10:14, How shall they believe in Him of whom they have not heard? And how shall they hear without a preacher? And how shall they preach, except they be sent? As it is written, *How beautiful are the feet of them that preach the gospel of peace*, and bring glad tidings of good things!"

The call of God should include a number of heart felt attitudes within the ministry. This includes a sure knowledge that God himself says, "How beautiful are the feet of them that preach the gospel." We who are truly called of God, and appointed and given by the Lord Jesus Christ himself as "gifts unto men" must consider ourselves blessed and honored. *It is a tremendous privilege to be called of God to the work of the ministry.* May this be our attitude.

In 1985, I was heading for a city wide crusade in a place called Ipil, in the province of Zamboanga Del Sur in the southern Philippines. I was taking the place of a brother who was slated to go but was not well enough to travel. Our small plane arrived about an hour late in the nearest airport to the east, a city called Pagadian. Because the plane was late, I missed the bus to Ipil, and went through the normal wrangling with a jeepney driver to persuade him to drive me there. (A jeepney is a locally made passenger truck.) The drive was a six hour affair over some very rough road. This was at a time when the "new peoples' army," a guerrilla group held responsible for killing and decapitating a large number of pastors in that area, were at the peak of their power.

A few other stranded citizens asked me if they could get a ride in my negotiated, captive jeepney. Among them was a young doctor and his wife, heading for their first assignment. While we traveled, he plied me with numerous questions. After talking for a while, he asked me if I knew of the MPA threat. I told him I did, and that I was a Christian missionary. Seeing my weariness, and the arduous travel over that difficult road, he said, "Sir, you have made a great sacrifice coming to the poverty of our country." I thought about his statement and answered him, "No, it is not a sacrifice, but a privilege." The young doctor thought for a moment and suddenly tears sprang into his eyes, as he understood my answer. Truly it is a privilege above all privileges and an honor above all honors to represent and serve the living God of heaven and earth and be called to the ministry. We worship you, our living God and Father of our Lord Jesus Christ.

A Right Spirit

The first thing a ministry needs is an awe and reverence for Almighty God. *He needs a deep sense of gratitude for his personal gift of salvation.* He needs a love, an inward adoration, and a spirit of worship towards our Savior Jesus Christ. Every ministry and child of God, needs a deep sense of reverence for the person of the Holy Spirit, who works within us, through us, and with us in our walk and ministry life.

There are a number of other ingredients that are also necessary within the man of God to affect a right spirit. We need to see the total Lordship of our Savior. This means a thorough knowledge that we are nothing without Him. He is our Lord in every area of our lives. We are not our own and we are bought with a price. We owe Him our all, our lives and our worship. This means that we bow to His ways, direction and desires. *Five-fold ministry cannot function and come into its own unless this is the case.* If those called to the ministry do not bow at Jesus' feet, they will not bow to His word!

If we are to present ourselves as the ministry of God, it is of utmost importance that we walk in a right spirit. This means that whatever we do in the name of the Lord should be done in the Spirit of the Lord. He is long suffering and gentle, slow to anger and plenteous in mercy. He is the fulfillment of all that is written of the fruit of the Spirit in Gal. 5:22. *Without a right spirit, one will never flow in a Godly Scriptural authority and church structure.* This right spirit begins manifesting in our lives when we yield ourselves totally to the Lordship of Jesus Christ, and when we acknowledge Him as our Lord and Savior.

He is the head of the church. *When we yield to Him, we will flow with Him and submit to Him first, as our main authority. Then we will submit to others that He places in the church and in our lives as unto Him.* This a is the same submission "as unto the Lord" wives owe their husbands (Eph. 5:22). To submit to their husbands is to submit to the Lord. Likewise, to submit to a proper and truly scriptural ministry, in reality, is to worship the Lord. We honor Him, and bow to His wisdom and dominion.

We will be tested in this matter, and it will be difficult, especially when the human nature of the people we deal with demonstrates less than a right spirit. Since all men are less than perfect, including us, submission is difficult at times, and calls for supernatural grace, wisdom, and patience. Submission includes—and even demands—a total reverence for His Word. We must search out of His desires in us and for us. This is the normal result of a spirit of worship for Him who died for us. Let us look at Ephesians 5:22 to 25, "Wives, be in subjection unto your own husbands, as unto the Lord. For the husband is the head of the wife, and Christ also is the head of the church, being himself the savior of the body. But as the church is subject to Christ, so let the wives also be to their husbands in everything. Husbands, love your wives, even as Christ also loved the church and gave himself up for it."

This scripture portrays Christian marriage, and in vserses 31 and 32, we find that this also includes the married couple becoming one flesh. This relationship is compared to Christ and the Church. This poses the requirement that wives submit unto their husbands as unto the Lord; when they submit to the authority structure required of them by the Lord, they in fact are submitting to Christ himself. In the same manner, we who submit to others in the church body with a right spirit, in reality are submitting to the Lord Jesus Christ. This passage categorically states that Christ is the head of the Church. By acknowledging this truth, we seek His direction and approval in our ministry walk. The Lord Jesus ordained order and an authority structure, in marriage, as well as in the church. Husbands are commanded to love their wives and give themselves up for them. Likewise may we give ourselves up for the church. We lay down our rights, and our lives.

To be a true servant of the Lord demands DEATH of self. God promises this will bring forth fruitfulness and life. " I am the true vine, and my Father is the husbandman. Every branch in me that beareth not fruit, He taketh it away: and every branch that beareth fruit, He cleanseth it, that it may bear more fruit. Already ye are clean because of the word which I have spoken unto you. Abide in me, and I in you. As the branch cannot bear fruit of itself, except it abide in the vine; so neither can ye, except ye abide in me" (John 15:1-4).

Abiding in Christ brings forth life and fruitfulness. This is painfully and painstakingly explained by the apostle Paul, bringing understanding to the young and budding ministry, Timothy.

In 2 Timothy 2:4 we read, "No man that warreth entangleth himself with the affairs of this life; that he may please Him who hath chosen him to be a soldier. And if a man also strive for masteries, yet is he not crowned, except he strive lawfully. The husbandman that laboureth must be first partaker of the fruits. Consider what I say; and *the Lord give thee understanding in all things. Remember that Jesus Christ of the seed of David was raised from the dead* according to my gospel."

This is strong. The apostle Paul is pointing out something every "Timothy" who enters the ministry should consider soberly. Jesus Christ the great husbandman died, before He rose from the dead and gave life to the church. You and I need to taste of death to self, before we bring forth life. This is another way of saying, "It is no longer I that liveth, but Christ that liveth in me." We need to face and experience death to self to really portray Jesus to the church and the people of this world. *To the degree that we do not demonstrate death to self and a right spirit, we limit The Lord Jesus Christ.*

Death to self, involves several basic steps. It begins with an acknowledgment within our selves that God's ways are higher than ours and wiser than ours. We read in Psalm 96:9 and 10, "Oh, worship the Lord in the beauty of holiness! Tremble before Him, all the earth. Say among the nations, "The Lord reigns.'" Within our being there should be a hallelujah and amen to that reading. Holiness should be beautiful, to the point that we will forsake a self life to attain it. Rev. David Derkson, from Surrey, British Columbia, Canada, pointed out to me that holiness means to be set apart *from* something, as well as being set apart *for* something. How true this is. We are set apart for the cause of the gospel and the building of the church of Jesus Christ.

This death means a death to our plans that do not conform to His plans, and certainly no plans would be made without seeking His face and approval. This death means limiting of our rights to self assertion, in attitude and self expression. All of this comes out of a spirit of worship, rather than by demand and works of the law.

Jesus exemplified this, when He pointed out His oneness with the Father. When His brothers in a mocking way told Him to go to the Feast of Tabernacles to show His works, He said in John 7:6 to 7, "My time has not yet come, but your time is always ready. The world cannot hate you, but it hates Me because I testify of it that its works are evil." Jesus said here that their times were their own. Why? Because they were unbridled and in control of their own person, and did whatever they felt like. Jesus said that His time had not come, meaning that He was not free to go. He was not directed yet, and was told to hold steady under the reign of God. Yet He went a few days later. He also said that they were of no offense to the world, and that He under the reign of God was.

There cannot be a true death to self without total worship and relinquishing of ourselves to Him who bought us with a price. We see this spirit demonstrated throughout the New Testament.

A Spirit of Unity

Beginning in the first chapter of Acts, even before Pentecost and the initial baptism of the Holy Spirit, we read, "These were in one accord and prayer." We do not see a spirit of competition here or a lack of regard one for another. If we want to know how the gospel explosion took place in the book of Acts, we need to pay attention to the larger considerations that birthed the church explosion. *We read twelve times that the people and multiple, five-fold ministry were in one accord.* Because the ministries were included in this statement, this really blesses me and gives me hope for today. This doubly blesses me when I consider that there was multiple ministry throughout the book of Acts, flowing together in one accord.

In Acts 2:42 and 43 they were under the (plural) apostles doctrine. In verse 46 the situation includes all of them being in one accord, including the original twelve apostles.

In 1 Corinthians 3:3, Paul points out that if division, strife, and envy are among them, they are carnal. Their division was demostrated by the attitude , "I am for Paul" and "I am for Apollos." Paul planted and Apolos watered, in the same garden of God, and God gave the increase (verse 6). This is the right spirit of one ministry towards another; Paul focuses on Apollos' place and value along with his own. *Today we divide Christ* (1 Cor. 1:13). In several ways, we in the ministry are more responsible for this than the congregation. We do not esteem our fellow ministry the way we should. Some will no doubt say "How can you tar me with a blanket brush? You are exempt from this blanket judgment only if you commonly invite other ministries into your setting, and have a multiple ministry in place. In chapter 3:23, Paul concludes with "Ye are Christ's," thereby signifying that *we are only servants of Christ. The church belongs to Him.*

In Galatians 1:10, Paul states that if we please men, then we are not servants of Christ. If we are truly and fully servants of Christ, we will esteem others that Jesus Christ has called to the ministry, and acknowledge our nakedness and incompleteness without them. Lord, forgive us for the pride of being lords over God's heritage. We say through our body language that we are complete in ourselves.

Consider Philippians 2:3, where Paul says, "Let nothing be done through vainglory, rather *esteem others better than your-selves." He prefaces this comment with "Be of one accord and one mind."* We will not have one accord until our minds hold and express this attitude. In 1 Corinthians 9:19, Paul says, "I am free from all men, yet I have made myself a servant to all." This includes our fellow ministry elders.

Without this attidtude of prefering one another, how can we

be of one accord? How can we be in the place where the oil flows down Aaron's garments? That is reserved for the brethren who dwell in unity, and truly desire the commanded blessing of the Lord (Ps. 133). This will be good and pleasant. Do we desire this?

A Right Spirit—Attitude

The spirit of man, his conscience, controls what the soul realm will do by approving and disapproving our plans and actions. Speaking about our martyred brother Stephen, Acts 6:8-10 says they "Could not resist the wisdom and spirit by which he spoke." Stephen was a man of faith who was used in the gift of miracles. This is speaking of his spirit, small s, totally yielded to the Lord. The Holy Spirit played a song on this world class violin that brings heaven itself to its feet (chapter 7:55b) What a yielded spirit.

Ananias exemplified this same spirit in Acts 9:13. He knew Saul as a persecutor and murderer, but he obeyed with the words "brother Saul" (verse 19). How much more should we who have the written word follow this example. We know Ephesians 4:11 to 13. Saul had that type of spirit. The moment he was knocked down and found out who Jesus really was, he immediately said, "What would you have me do, Lord?" Just a few days later we find him preaching Christ in the synagogues (verse 20).

What a response to the call of God. Perhaps ZEAL is a heart, soul, mind, and spirit yielded to the Holy Spirit. We find that John the Baptist was filled with the Holy Ghost from his mother's womb, and came in the spirit and power of Elijah (Lk. 1:15,17). Do the scriptures not say of Jesus that "The zeal of God's house has eaten me up." He was consumed with zeal for the temple of God—you and me. Talk about a right spirit!

In Acts 16:6 to 7, Paul was forbidden of the Holy Ghost to go somewhere. He was listening for Holy Ghost direction. Because of this he did not miss the Macedonian call. A right spirit seeks direction.

Look at Acts 16:3, where Paul circumcised Timothy, the young man he loved in the Lord. Did Paul not understand the pain and humiliation that he would cause the young man? Did he not teach in Galatians 5:2 and 3, that if one was to be circumcised

Christ would profit him nothing, and that he would be a debtor to the whole law? *Talk about a right spirit.* He did this thinking of the offense that he would cause to the gospel, but realized how much he would limit himself and the gospel if he did not do it. Unless Timothy was circumcized, he would not even get a chance to present the gospel to these intended converts. Think of Timothy, of whom Paul eventually said that he had no man like him. Small wonder. Think of the sacrifice of praise that went up when he submitted himself to this procedure with a Godly intent.

Powerful examples of a right spirit abound in the New Testament. Certainly Paul and Silas singing in prison after being beaten for the gospel's sake in Acts 16:25 is one of them. There was no room for a self-pity party, only a right focus. The elders in Acts 20 also demonstrated this attitude. They dropped whatever they were doing, and went when the apostle ministry asked them to.

Some of the scriptural examples are a little hard when you really try to apply them to your self. I read Acts 17:16 that Paul's spirit was stirred within him at the sight of ungodliness and idolatry. I ask myself , Is my spirit stirred within me as I view the events of today? In another example found in chapter 19:30, Paul would have entered in, even in the face of violence and pain, to help a hurting brother. In 21:13, he said that he was ready to die for the cause of Christ. Could I say that? Lord, create a right spirit within me.

A Right Spirit is Gentle and Caring

We see this truth exemplified in numerous places. In Rom. 15:1 we read, "We that are strong ought to be caring for and supporting the weak." This is totally acting in consideration of others. This is looking at someone who is weaker than ourselves and being considerate of their needs. That is true ministry. That is the opposite of a power and authority figure awareness, which so often prevails. In fact, James said this in different words, "Pure religion and undefiled *before God the Father* is to visit the fatherless and the widow in their affliction" (James 1:27). This is the opposite of what Jesus taught about "Pharisee ministry." Pharisees prayed in public to be seen. How is your prayer life?

Pharisees gave in public, and demanded the highest seats.

In Acts 16:40 we see Paul comforting the Philippian church. A sermon can be preached from Acts 20:7. What an example of a caring heart! We find Paul preaching out of a heart of burden, knowing he was leaving the next day. He preached until midnight, and with a slight pause to raise the dead, he spoke until day break. Are we truly called of God? Have we made our calling and election sure? Can we say as he did in verse 19, that we have served the Lord and not men with all humility and tears? Do we ever weep for the right reasons? As Paul said in verse 20, have we taught our people all that is profitable for them, and not that which tickled their ears and amused them? The result may be that people fall on our necks and weep sorely, if they heard we are leaving them (verse 37).

In 1 Corinthains 16:24, we read, "Greet one another with a holy kiss." Today this is seldom seen in attitude, and never mind reality. If the ministries would truly exemplify this attitude one toward another, it might reach into the congregation. Get rid of a self righteous critical spirit if this applies to you. Paul says this in a blunt, straight forward way in 1 Corinthians 16:24 when he says "My love be with you." May my love be with you as well, Paul. I want to meet you in heaven, right after I see Jesus. Maybe there are some Pauls around, right here on earth. Are you one of them?

In 2 Corinthians 7:12 Paul says, "Our care for you in the sight of God." Are we truly aware of our spiritual stewardship, which deserves and demands care in the sight of God? Do people view us as a learned Reverend, a super spiritual person and untouchable? Are we an honored leader, and a knowledgeable teacher, *or* an elder brother, with a father's heart, full of love and compassion? Paul knew this demanded a caring attitude, as he expressed in 2 Corinthians 10:1. *"I beseech you by the meekness and gentleness of Christ."*

In Galatians 4:19, Paul says, "My little children," and that was not demeaning. He goes on, "I travail in birth again until Christ be formed in you." Is that our attitude? If someone accepts Christ in our ministry environment, will we see that the new child is instantly breast fed, comforted, and encouraged? Or do we simply hope that they will turn up the next Sabbath day?

Ephesians 4:2 that we are to forbear one another in love, in all lowliness, with long-suffering and meekness. There have been times in my ministry experience that I was made to feel like a disease walked in the door by the ministry in charge when I visited some churches. Maybe we do not all belong to the same ministerial affiliation, but we are serving the same Lord! Ministries should always acknowledge and welcome visiting ministries. Several times in my personal experience, I have felt cold suspicion, and the hard eye that said I was not welcome. Many others I know would tell similar or worse stories.

In Philippians 2:20, Paul complimented Timothy, *who naturally cared for the state of the believers in Philippi*. This is a rare value, even in his day, and Paul knew no one else this could be said of. What a contrast to the next verse, where "all seek their own." What an indictment! LORD JESUS, may I have a right spirit. In my ministry walk, may I not seek my own.

We can not leave this point without focusing on 1 Thessalonians 2:7 and 8. Here Paul says that he and Silvanus and Timothy, his fellow apostles, were gentle among the people, as a nurse cherisheth her children. What a word picture. Sometimes we are blessed to observe a baby being fed at it's mothers breast. Truly, this is one of life's most beautiful pictures of bliss and contentment in the face of mother and child. This is what Paul is referring to. This picture is destroyed when I think of times that I have seen ministries beating up their people over collections and finances. I even remember one who held the people in the grip of fear and would not dismiss them until they gave an amount that satisfied him in a second or third offering. I divorced myself from this ministry for this and other things.

I think of a prophetess who was truly used in the gift of prophecy, who got into an attitude of the wrath of God while prophesying until I can not bear to hear the words, they grate on my spirit so much. I weep at the thought of the wrong projected into the lives of hearers who may be weak in understanding. Their opinion of God will suffer. Some will no doubt follow the bad example. One that really rips my heart is the story told by an elderly man who was present as I ministered at a local retirement home. After I spoke, he told me weeping that his wife had recently passed away following a three year long illness. The thing which hurt him most were the words of the "pastor" he was involved with for many years. He asked that pastor, "How come you only stopped in to see her a couple of times in three years to pray with her during her suffering?" He replied, "That is not my job."

A Spirit of Servanthood

The risen savior told Peter, "If you love me feed my sheep and my lambs, my little ones." He is saying the same to you and me. To say we love Him means we will serve Him. James, Peter, and Paul introduced themselves as servants after that they stated their callings. Help us, Lord, to truly understand what that means, and how it is to be acted out in our lives when dealing with the sheep, little ones, and our fellow elders.

We find in Romans 12:10 that we are to honor and prefer one another in brotherly love. This calls for true humility. May we desire a right spirit, that like the elders in Revelation. We must cast our crowns,and all that we are down before Him. who is worthy to receive all glory, power, and honor. Praise His Holy name.

A Submissive Spirit is a Right Spirit

We first submit to God, and then to man as unto the Lord. In Acts 4:23 Peter and John reported their experiences and recent events to their own company. They did not plan and act independently, but exemplified a spirit of submission to the plurality. We see this spirit of submission to Christ in Acts 5:20 and 21. Following an abusive event, they obeyed the commandment of Christ, making themselves vulnerable to further abuse. Then in verse 29 they faced threatening authorities and told them that they were to obey God rather then men. May we today take that statement to heart.

We find a balancing statement from Paul in Galatians 2:6, where he says, "But they who seemed to be somewhat, it makes no matter to me, for God accepts no man's person." He clearly says that he was not going to give obeisance to those who thought they were somebody and demanded a wrong submission.

May it be said of us, and may we be able to say with Paul, "But you have carefully followed my doctrine, manner of life, purpose, faith, long-suffering, love, perseverance, persecutions, (as well as) afflictions" (2 Tim. 3:10).

Lord Jesus, be the Lord of my life. Heavenly Father, I come to you in Jesus' name and worship you, almighty God. Holy spirit, may we not grieve you. Create in me a right spirit, My Lord and my God.

Chapter 9

MULTIPLE AND FIVE-FOLD MINISTRY FLOW

Only a right spirit in the ministries involved will allow multiple ministry to become a reality in the church. *Why is this the main basic ingredient?* Because with a right spirit, each one will bow to the word of our Lord out of simple obedience, whether he understands it fully or not. Ministries will accept that they are only one part of His gift ministries. The New Testament in Ephesians 4:8 clearly says the Lord gave gifts unto men, plural. Specifically, He gave apostles, prophets, evangelists, pastors, and teachers.

With a right spirit ministries will accept the fact that they are incapable of seeing in full measure and need what the other person's abilities and insights. They will accept the fact that they have not been given the same sight and insight. This realization will affect any ministry's attitude towards another; they will see their need to accept other ministries. This takes faith in the Word of God, and not leaning unto our own understanding.

With a right spirit, ministries will accept that others have been given abilities that they do not have, or our Lord Jesus would not have given other ministries differing from our callings. When presented with the scene in Acts 13:1, where a multiple number of ministries were waiting on God, they will immediately become convicted. They would immediately discern the discrepancy between this holy scene and today. They will agree that a multiple ministry in a spirit of unity is God's desire and example of what is right, and anything less is deficient, immature, and born of a wrong spirit or ignorance. If we see this and do not desire change, we are guilty of willful ignorance and rebellion.

With a right spirit, ministries will acknowledge they are incomplete. Rather than walk in a spirit of independence and self

105

sufficiency, they will desire a servant of the Lord Jesus Christ attitude. They will place less value on themselves and their position. We humbly bow at your feet, our Savior God, and by love will serve one another.

With a right spirit, they will desire the fulfillment of Ephesians 4:13, and desire that the church come to maturity. They will acknowledge with humility that they are insufficient to see this happen on their own, since we are incomplete.

With a right spirit, they will not only cease walking in the pride of their own conceits and self sufficiency, but *will cry out to God for the other parts* of the fully God given ministry. Each one will cry, "I am naked. I need the blessing and deposit and equipping of my fellow ministers. My people need this."

With a right spirit, we will repent of selfish pride, spiritual ambition, and "solo ministry."

IS THIS NOT SO? I challenge you to be a Berean and to be more noble than those who will not take the time. Examine the scriptures. Try to find a church in the New Testament that had less than multiple ministry. Consider also that a multiple ministry is not necessarily a proper, functional five-fold ministry. You may have a variety of callings together in one place, but without God's order. Without understanding the importance of this, you still will not have a functional, complete five-fold ministry as God intended. This is a step in the right direction. Let's see why this is so, and examine the effect.

Our Example

In the New Testament church, beginning with the book of Acts, we find an explosion of the gospel. The good news of salvation spread under the flames and fanning of the Holy Ghost, until one observed in their day, "These that have turned the world upside down are come hither also. The whole world is gone after them" (Acts 17:6). We see in the light of scriptures and history that they made a remarkable dent into the unbelief of their known world.

Had the gospel continued to progress at the same rate of speed as it advanced in the first century, the whole world would have been reached long ago. If we use common mathematics to chart the potential advance of their progress, we have an awesome picture. Had other factors not deterred this growth, we would see the world touched completely several times over. Over the next ninety-eight years, they covered ten times the territory that was reached by year two after Pentecost. That is a conservative assessment. Had they covered ten times the area reached at the end of the first century by the second century, and did that again by the end of the hundred years, the world would easily have been reached by the end of the third century.

Let's examine three things that made their achievements possible, and the changes that crippled this profound growth.

•Existing and Change. The church began with a holy endowment of power accompanied by manifestations of the supernatural, and ushered in by the baptism of the Holy Spirit. This baptism was done away with doctrinally and subsequently experientially because of the unbelief associated with wrong teaching. As a result, the supernatural gifts of the Holy Spirit did not operate. The church no longer saw things like Peter's shadow healing ministry in Acts 5:15, or Stephen stunning the crowds with a Holy demonstration of unction and miracles (Acts 6:8), or Paul seeing a whole town converted due to the ministry of the Holy Spirit through him (Acts 28:8).

The body of Christ was no longer strengthened by prophetic, revelatory ministry. In Acts 11:28, Agabus spoke forth a future happening to prepare the church; in Acts 21:10, he ministered to Paul, which probably had an affect on his resolve. After the first century, church history, no longer says the Holy Ghost was working with them, confirming the word with signs and miracles. We know the Holy Ghost was there, bringing conviction of sin, sanctification and comfort, but the supernatural was lost. Faith in God's word will bring it back.

•Existing and Change. The church began with a clear, identified multiple ministry. We read about evangelist, prophet, teacher and apostle ministries interacting and functioning. This multiple ministry was obliterated in the years following the first century. Instead many names were attached to clergy, who often did not even know Christ. (Read Fox's *Book of Martyrs.*) *Faith in God's word will bring the multiple ministry back.*

• Existing and Change. The church began with order and authority in the functioning of the total ministry, so the five-fold ministry functioned and flowed under apostolic headship. Church growth was moving rapidly and solidly under the foundation ministries of apostles and prophets (Eph. 2:20). There was a clear regard for the various ministries by all the others, and work was headed up by apostles (1 Cor. 12:28). According to history, this order was destroyed, and we saw a massive decline of growth as a result. *Faith in and a holy regard for God's word will bring this order back.*

Five-Fold Ministry Flow

The book of Acts begins with a powerful series of events. It began with a group of believers in faith, humility of spirit, and unity praying and waiting in obedience on God. They had already received the Spirit (John 20:22), and were waiting in obedience (Acts 1:4) for the baptism of their spirit man into the Holy Spirit by the Lord Jesus Christ (John 1:33). This is what it will take to get the same power today (Acts 1:8). *Believe that.*

The Holy Ghost descended and the Lord Jesus baptized their spirits in the Holy Spirit. I have yet to meet the person who sincerely set out in like manner who did not receive like results. This was the birth of what followed.

As this supernatural picture unfolded, we see peoples and unbelievers drawn in, as they get saved hearing Peter's sermon. We see the principles of church growth set out in Acts 2:40, and we see the apostles taking a leading role in portraying the gospel to their world. We also see the raising up, growth, and the directing of ministries through the Apostles. There is no other portrayal to be found in the New Testament.

As offense was caused by their bold witness to the world and to the religious system, which is normal wherever the true gospel is portrayed, persecution began. Peter and John raised a lame man in the name of Jesus Christ of Nazareth, and that miracle caused a gospel tidal wave, along with persecution. Stephen preached a pointed, powerful sermon with a face that was transformed by the inner glory, and had a gift ministry of powerful miracles. They killed him. Today it is no different. The child of the flesh still persecutes the child of the Spirit. In Acts 8:4-5, the gospel spreads. The Apostles immediately follow up the newly saved, establishing the converts (8:14). First the apostle delegation saw to it that the new believers were baptized in the Holy Ghost, then established the new church. Again in Acts 11:22, the Jerusalem apostles sent out the apostle Barnabas to deal with the believers. They had heard reports that the scattered believers had been fruitful, and gave Barnabas a mandate to establish the new saints.

We then see this picture in more detail as we follow the apostles Paul and Barnabas. They set out and portray church planting as it was meant to be. If we would follow this example be followed we would have similar results today.

They had a great springboard and the right setting for the birth of their work. In Acts 13:1 we see multiple believers, just as we did in Acts 2. In this case they were all ministries, waiting on the Lord with a spirit of unity, willing to do whatever the Lord of heaven and earth desired. Each had the ability to hear the Holy Ghost and the correct spirit to follow his directions. We see these two apostles, neither one being part of the original twelve, set out under the direct command of the Holy Ghost. And then we see the churches being established, out of the raw materials of new believers. Right from the beginning of their trip, and everywhere they went, Paul and Barnabus ordained elders and established the churches. Most of the rest of the New Testament are writings to these very churches that Paul and Barnabas, as well as Titus and some others, established.

THE WHOLE THING BEGAN WITH THE MINISTRY OF ACCEPTED APOSTLES. In most of the accounts, establishing churches was done by apostles other than the initial twelve, and *that should tell us something. Have you ever considered why?* We see our Lord Jesus devoting half of his three year public ministry on these first twelve apostles, preparing them for the work ahead. Yet the foundation gospel work was done by apostles other than the first twelve. Paul tells what happened to him after his salvation in Galatians chapter one. He went to Arabia and Damascus for the first three years and then spent fifteen days with Peter in Jerusalem. He did not return there for fourteen more years. In verse seventeen, he specifically states he did not confer with the apostles that were before him.

I believe there were numerous apostles called that had and have nothing to do with the Jerusalem twelve, just as there are today. I believe the Lord of Glory intentionally had the scriptures record the church growth by other than the first twelve. He knew the scriptural understanding and example would die, and left us a pointer back to the right way. We do find a couple of instances in the first twelve chapters of Acts where the initial twelve apostles were involved in establishing church foundations. After that, ninety-eight percent of the church planting was done by other apostles, such as Barnabas, Titus, Timothy, Paul and more.

Before his ascension, Jesus said he would build his church on the apostles, specifically on Peter, whose name meant stone or rock. Paul pointed out in Ephesians 2:20 that the church is built on the foundation of apostles and prophets, with Jesus Christ as the chief apostle and corner stone. Why apostles and prophets? What is different about these ministries?

APOSTLES and PROPHETS have a larger world vision. APOSTLES establish, gather, and set in order. Usually the pastor is the other ministry with the ability to gather. That is why you see so many pastors leading churches. Pastors do not have a burning zeal, burden or vision for the territory over the horizon. They do not have a burden to see multiple other ministries raised up. Look at ninety-nine out of one hundred pastor-led churches if you need proof. They do not have the general's view of the battle. They are not given that vision and are not first, second, or third in church authority, but somewhere after that. I love my pastor brethren, but find it even easier to love them when they do not display egotistical flesh or disregard their fellow ministries and God's order. It's easy to see we need pastors, and JESUS gave them to us. However, when pastors control the local church, they hold the assets belonging to God. By taking wrongful authority over these assets, they keep the gospel from going into all the world. They take a job that is not theirs, and which they have not been equipped for. They limit God by not flowing with His desired authority structure. (1 Cor. 12:28)

These assets are much greater than finances. Often have I attended a church where I see by revelation that many have a zeal and burden to enter into some form of ministry and are stifled.

The pastor in control did not see the work of the Holy Spirit in their hearts. He did not have an apostle or prophet's desire and gift to lead them. Allow an apostle or prophet ministry to share his burden and vision with the congregation, and let him ask the congregation if they would like to be part of a team ministering overseas. Now watch the response. If you give him the place Christ intended him to have, the apostle will spur growth in ministry.

Often the scenario goes like this. Having been thoroughly drilled about submission to him, some spirit filled sister asks the pastor if it would be all right to accompany an overseas ministry on a mission. She is promptly reminded of her responsibilities to her Sunday school class and the dangers involved in such a trip, instead of the tremendous opportunity to serve God and the Kingdom. I realize there is more to this, such as relationships of trust with another ministry, but the difference in burden does apply. Financial focus is another matter.

Take the foundation apostles and prophets out of the place God intended them to be, and you cripple church growth. In their proper place, they will discern other young ministries, and motivate them. They will impart vision to gospel workers and those whom God is calling to the ministry. "Many are called and few are chosen" applies here as well (Math. 22:14). The functional foundation ministries will motivate baby ministries and impart Holy Ghost vision.

Look at Romans 1:1, where Paul identifies himself and his calling under God. He continues this thought in verse 5, pointing out some specifics that are natural to his heart and calling. As you observe him through the window of this text, you clearly see the normal heart, desire, and work of the Holy Spirit in any mature apostle. He received apostleship—he did not take it upon himself—for obedience to the faith in all nations. He was called to minister to saints in all nations. He writes to the Rome church, which he did not establish, and tells the eldership and adherents that he has enough of a burden for them that he prays for them without ceasing, even though he never met them. He tells this leadership that he has not yet met that he intends to stop in and minister to their church. *Try that today!* Furthermore, he unabashedly tells them that he wants to impart some Spiritual gift unto them, and minister in such a way as to establish them. Most churches and ministries I know today would say, "He wants to do what? What does he think is wrong with us? He is not even one of our ministries. Our church is established. We have been in this place for thirty years and have gone through three pastors, and all of them good men. We even added on to the building a few years ago, and have an increased membership." Some apostles today with a God given burden for a church work have been denied and turned down by the ministry in charge, and in reality, the Lord Jesus Christ was turned down.

We see Paul pouring out his heart and he naturally expects those leaders to receive him. *If Rome denies him, they deny Christ and the work of the Holy Spirit in Paul.* Think about it! The same applies today!

Consider and Take Note

We see the seeds of this wrong spirit and attitude prophesied by Paul before he left his place in the Ephesian church. "For I know this, that after my departing shall grievous wolves enter in among you, not sparing the flock. Also of your own selves shall men arise, speaking perverse things, to draw away disciples after them. Therefore watch, and remember, that by the space of three years I ceased not to warn every one night and day with tears" (Acts 20:29-31).

This applies much more today when most people do not understand that some are called as apostles. Those that do understand cannot identify those apostles. Of those few that can identify them, even fewer allow them their place. Paul was a defensive wall, and he knew it would go down when he left. He knew there would be no replacement for himself, for some reason, or he would not have said that. Probably the ministries in charge at a later point refused the foundation apostle ministry, because I have no doubt that the Lord of the church would have provided it.

I clearly recall an outreach ministry group under a traveling prophet. This prophet visited and ministered every other week. By invitation, I ministered there, traveling several hundred miles. After the first evening of ministry, I asked the prophet about two men sitting at the back. I had never met either one, but I told him to eliminate them from his meetings or they would destroy his work. A year later I was again involved in the same place, and again identified these same two men to the prophet with the strongest warning I could communicate. He looked at the growth of the group and the first elder in place and ignored my words. Approximately six months later the elder called and requested that I hold some meetings, saying that there had been a decline of attendance. I came early to hear and see the activities of their Friday night teaching meeting. At the front was one of those two men. Before the man got passed his introduction, I stood up and told him and those present by revelation that the speaker in veiled terms was teaching them against the doctrine of the deity of Christ. I told the elder that I could not keep silent or minister there if he allowed this. The second man of the two then stood up out of the congregation, debating the doctrine of the deity of Christ. The elder, who was a spirit-baptized man with clear doctrines a year before this, would not separate with these men over this corner stone doctrine. The work was destroyed. To the best of my knowledge, the prophet has never acknowledged this Godly warning or repented of his sin.

Apostles are a defense against wolves, and yet are often refused today. One might say such a statement is rather pre-sumptuous. Observe and see the seeds of this even in Paul's day. In 2 Corinthians 7:2 , he pleaded with the Corinthians to "receive us."

We also see this written by the "love apostle," John, when he said in 3 John 1:9 to 11, *"I wrote unto the church: but Diotrephes, who loves to have the preeminence among them, receives us not. Wherefore, if I come, I will remember his deeds which he does, prating against us with malicious words: and not content therewith, neither does he himself receive the brethren, and forbids them that would, and casts them out of the church.* Beloved, follow not that which is evil."

This all too often appears to be the case today. Diotrephes had a long family tree succeeding him. It is clear that this type of evil, ignorance, and departure from truth grew, but God is restoring his church in this hour!

We see a different spirit in many churches in the book of Acts, such as in chapter 11:26-27, where the apostles and prophets were received by the church of Antioch. Small wonder supernatural direction in Antioch was possible, clearly directing the affairs of ministries that changed the course of history (Chapter 13:1-3) Likewise in Chapter 12:25, Paul and Barnabas were received in Jerusalem. Again in Antioch, in chapter 14:26, we see that Paul and Barnabas were received and stayed there and taught there for a long time. Other ministries and elders in place made room for them. Also in Chapter 15:30 to 35 we see that Judas and Silas, Jerusalem prophets, were also received and ministered there. What a church! I want to be part of a modern day Antioch. Again in Acts 21:17 we see that the Jerusalem apostles and elders received Paul and Barnabas gladly.

The Beginning of the Church

The apostle Peter led off with the first sermon and three thousand souls got saved (Acts 2:14). We see the church grow and take off from there. This growth is described by nine *ands*, beginning with verse 42.

1] *And* they continued steadfastly in the apostles' doctrine and fellowship, in the breaking of bread.

2] *And* in prayers. Then fear came upon every soul,

3] *And* many wonders and signs were done through the apostles. Now all who believed were together,

4] *And* had all things in common,

5] *And* sold their possessions and goods,

6] *And* divided them among all, as anyone had need. So continuing daily with one accord in the temple,

7] *And* breaking bread from house to house, they ate their food with gladness and simplicity of heart, praising God

8] *And* having favor with all the people.

9] *And* the Lord added to the church daily those who were being saved.

The people did great when they were under the authority ministry of the apostles. Signs and miracles were a common happening (verse 43). There was a doctrine diet that brought great results, and birthed a spirit of love for one another that actually touched deep enough to affect their wallets. The apostles Peter and John were used of God to heal a lame man in Acts 3:4, and that miracle had a profound affect.

In chapter five we see tough love, when the apostle Peter brought judgment on deceitful people, and the affect was holiness in the church, and more growth. In chapter 6:2 we see the apostles setting things in order, and appointing deacons in the church, who administered the financial affairs and needs of the church. These deacons were set free to minister in the lives and needs of people, and not merely delegated to count collections. In chapter 8:5 to 14, when the apostles heard how Philip the evangelist had ministered and brought salvation to Samaria, they immediately sent an apostolic delegation to establish the new converts.

In Acts 11:1 we see that when the apostles and brethren in Judaea heard the gentiles had received the gospel, they sent the apostle Barnabas to deal with this. The Judean apostles did not have any problems with this, but Peter had some explaining to do to the Jerusalem apostles and church, who were careful about his theology, questioning his spending time among the gentiles. Acts 13:1 stirs my heart. Here we see several ministries in one accord, waiting on the Lord and praying together. The Holy Ghost spoke and commissioned two apostles to their ministry work. These two promptly set out and blazed a trail of churches, setting elders in place over these new infant works, and in time visiting them again and again, establishing them and strengthening them. When Paul could not visit them, he wrote letters of teaching, comfort and direction to them with an elder's and father's heart.

All along the way we see miracles. We see healings in Acts chapter 14, and later a picture of submission to other apostles and elders in Jerusalem in questions of theology. Elders were set in place in Acts 14:23, and we read in Acts 16:5, "SO WERE THE CHURCHES ESTABLISHED." May we see this again today. May we see the church functioning under apostle ministry in doctrine, and a multiple, true, ministering, ordained eldership placed in every church.

We also see the battles with those who were moved with

envy, and a continual ministry of confrontation with those of the religious hierarchy (Acts 17:5). That seemed to be a consistent part of the apostles' ministry, along with the glory and power gifts, but through it all, the gates of hell did not prevail. The violent took the Kingdom by force, and the church was built! Perhaps Paul's handkerchief and apron ministry had something to do with the explosion of faith (Acts 19:12). I am convinced that the raising of the dead man in Acts 20:10 had a lasting impression on those believers.

Then in Acts 21 we see Paul fellowshipping with the evangelist Philip (verse 8). Hallelujah! We also see the prophet Agabus stopping in to catch some of this quality fellowship, made up of an apostle, an evangelist, four ladies that prophesied, and a now a prophet. Hallelujah! And as we often see today when the true prophet is received in the name of a prophet, the prophet blessed Paul with his gift and strengthened his walk.

What a picture we see in Acts 21:17! The Jerusalem ministry and church received Paul and his ministry company gladly. No spirit of competition or jealousy here. No distrust, no questions except whether he was of Christ. No struggle with an empire vision. No hint of struggle over of a financial question. Just a receiving with joy. More than that, he actually got to share what the Lord had done in his ministry, including the miracles, and they (verse 20), glorified God (verse 20). No an attitude of, "Do not share that or you will make me look bad," or worse yet, "I don't believe you." Just praise to God and joy. What a picture. THIS IS THE WAY IT SHOULD BE!

We see the apostles, with a burden and vision that is larger than the local church, governing affairs, and received and upheld in honor. We see the prophet, the other foundation ministry, traveling among the churches, sometimes together with the apostle. By their burden, vision, gifting, they brought the mind of the Lord to the church leaders and congregations. Flowing in the supernatural and revelation arenas, they established the hearts of the believers. We see the teacher, mighty in scripture, bringing maturity to the saints by the washing of the water of the Word. We see the evangelist reaching out with salvation to all, and the pastors, as the Lord gave them, serving among the elders and taking heed of the flock over which the Holy Ghost had placed them. We see a continual establishing of churches under elders, and a plurality of elders and ministries every time, as we read in Acts 20:28 and Titus 1:5. We see all of these ministries flowing, interacting, complementing each other, and making room for each other.

Take the apostle away from that picture, and you limit the growth and spread of the church. Take the prophet away as well, and you cut the establishing and strengthening, and minimize world church vision. You have destroyed the foundations and the master builders. "What about us?" say the pastors who today control the authority of most of the evangelical and full gospel churches. Most of you have not recognized these foundation ministries, or made room for them. When they came, you looked on them as competition and pushed them out. *Repent!* You who have seen but despised the teacher as less than yourself, *repent!*

"For thus saith the Lord. I will again establish my church as in the beginning, and restore all things before that great and mighty day of The Lord. You who have not made room for your fellow ministries, repent. You who have usurped the authority and lorded over God's heritage, repent! For this is the day of restoration."

This is God's normal church. Acts 13 is a normal situation, where teachers, prophets, and apostles, wait on the Lord and flow together. What a picture of unity. No wonder the oil flowed. "Behold, how good and how pleasant it is for brethren to dwell together in unity! It is like the precious ointment upon the head, that ran down upon the beard, even Aaron's beard: that went down to the skirts of his garments; As the dew of Hermon, and as the dew that descended upon the mountains of Zion: for there the LORD commanded the blessing, even life for evermore (Ps. 133:1-3).

No wonder prophetic direction came forth. I long for such a church. My heart cries out to God for such a place, where brethren esteem each other better than self, and make room for the blessing of the ministry of the other person, and benefit from the deposit of the anointing and gifting of Christ within our fellow ministry. A place where there is a shunning of empire vision and the approval of man. A place where there is a kingdom vision, and ministry to the orphan and the widow. A place where the little ones are fed. A place where deacons are not peanut counters, but filled with the Holy Ghost to serve in the area of needs. A place where the prayer of Jesus is answered. "And now I am no more in the world, but these are in the world, and I come to thee. Holy Father, keep through thine own name those whom thou hast given me, that they may be one as we are one" (John 17:11).

In 2 Corinthians 6:1-13, we find Paul makes a plea to the church. After saying that he and other ministers had opened their hearts to them, he asks that they might be enlarged and respond in like measure. In 2 Corinthians 7:2, he pleads, "Receive us." May we see and hear the plea and desire of our fellow ministries.

Praise God for the examples given to us, such as in Gal. 2:9. James, Cephas, and John, perceived the grace that was given to Paul, and gave him and Barnabas the right hands of fellowship. May we learn from Paul's attitude towards a fellow minister called Epaphras. In Colossians 1:7, he calls Epaphras "our dear fellow servant, who is for you a faithful minister of Christ." We also see this attitude expressed in return by that faithful minister of Christ in verse 8, where Epaphras "declared unto us your love in the Spirit." In Colossians 4:7 we read of "Tychicus a beloved brother, and a faithful minister and fellow servant in the Lord." In verse 9 we have Onesimus, a faithful and beloved brother. This is the attitude of Paul, who would probably be considered a successful minister by most people. Help us, Lord, to attain unto this height and grace of character.

The foundation ministries were loved and welcomed any time, and did not inconvenience the local elders' sermon series. With their oversight, and with the balance of elder ministries, we see a flourishing church allowing for many other functional ministries. These included helps, governments, deacons and "Dorcas" ministries. Included in this ministry picture we see a wonderful army of saints, God's Ambassadors. These have the benefit and training of the complete banquet table of God, which includes all five specific callings. With a maturity heading towards the measure of Jesus Christ himself, they are commissioned and sent out and released to do the work of the ministry. (Eph. 4:11-13) Wow! Lets have it! Lets reach the world!

118

"THOU ART WORTHY OH LORD. FOR THOU HAST REDEEMED US OUT OF EVERY KINDRED, TRIBE AND NATION." Even so, come quickly Lord Jesus.

Chapter 10

AUTHORITY, RESPONSIBILITY AND SUBMISSION, AND THE WILL OF MAN

Godly Authority

Praise God for being a wonderful God of order. We see this demonstrated in creation and in all God does. In Psalm 19, David pointed out that the heavens declare the glory of God. We see God's order in times and seasons, sun, moon, and stars, and in growth, with first the kernel, then the bud, then the plant and ear, then the full grown corn. We see this in heaven when it comes to ranks and authorities of angels, and in this world, when man was given dominion over all the earth. We still see this in the earth, as God sets up kings and removes kings and nations.

With order, there is also a need for authority and responsibility attached to authority. Authority at any level was never intended to be a power trip. God given authority is always to be applied with a total Godly sense of responsibility, and never apart from the character and nature of God. God cares for us, and we need to have a caring gentle attitude towards the flock. With the authority, there must be an application of the nature and image of God. God himself made order out of chaos, with a love and sensitivity, and a perception of color, individuality, detail, and personality. One green plant designed to flourish and blossom in sunshine, and another green plant designed to flourish in shade. Each has its place.

As a church under God, this should also be seen in the body of Christ. Paul said in 1 Corinthians 14:40, "Let all things be done decently and in order." This statement is applied to the governing of the church service, or how to conduct ourselves when we assemble together to meet before God. This decent order cannot be achieved and maintained without authorities in place.

Likewise, there are clear and defined guidelines in the New Testament, describing church government, and the church authority structure under God. This authority is to be demonstrated with all the love and care that Jesus himself portrayed. This spiritual structure is to operate both within and beyond the four walls of our local church buildings. *Take out the role and scriptural callings of apostles, prophets, and teachers, and you have a crippled and deficient church structure. I guarantee you will have less than what the scriptures portray, and this affects the growth of the gospel and church in the world.* In large measure, this is the cause of the difference between the book of Acts and the church today.

There are a number of church groups and denominations with a variety of centralized governments. None of these accurately portray the New Testament and God's holy structure without a clear understanding of *callings and foundation ministries.* The callings of apostle and prophet have a larger world vision. They should head up the church government, and their inclusion naturally focuses on taking the gospel into all the world (Math. 28:19). This is how the church achieves Matthew 24:14 and reaches all the world.

The closest large church government system I am aware of is a group that has regulations limiting those who are capable of functioning in the highest place of authority. They must have "mission fields" experience for a minimum period of years. To a large measure they are acting out what the Bible set out to accomplish, since most of these were probably apostles and prophets. They did not spell out and understand that the ministry must be an apostle but since the authority figure was involved in missions, he may have been an apostle or prophet. A prophetess started their organization, and they have maintained a strong missionary focus. An apostle at the helm of leadership will steer the ship with a different natural focus than a pastor.

In any case, they are still short of the New testament pattern. You do not vote callings in and out. They are Holy Ghost equipped, and He makes them what they are. You may have to discern between people who have the same calling as to maturity and which is the "elder Brother," but the facts of the New Testament pattern do not change, in regard to what Christ desires.

Submission

The very word *submission* sends chills up and down many spines. The reason is that few have seen Godly, balanced leadership. Many more shouldhave scare chills running up and down their spines if they really understood clearly what the nice guy at the top really represents, by design or ignorance. Many in leadership direct people to trust them and the church structure with their eternal souls, rather than Jesus. They do not direct their people as Paul did, to "be ye followers of me, even as I am of Christ" (1 Cor. 11:1). Few would say, "Examine my walk and do not follow me if you do not see me following Christ." May we in authority never try to take the wrong place in peoples lives, but always strive to press believers into Christ. If this goal be accomplished, the church could burn down and you pass on to glory, but *the saints would still stand.*

Some in the church fear authority and submission to a degree that they shun any genuine God-given and authority. Others are insecure in their faith, and want too much authority in their lives, often shunning responsibility for their personal walk with God. We can see a ditch on either side of the road, and aim to stay in the center of the road. Too much authority is one ditch; denying scriptural authority in the body of Christ is another. Let's review some scriptures that will help us avoid both ditches.

Scriptural authority can readily be supported by numerous scriptures, one of which is Hebrews 13:17. "Obey them that have the rule over you, and submit yourselves: for they watch for your souls, as they that must give account." Clearly there are some that have been given a place of ruling over others. We need to put scriptural submission on one side of the scale, and balance it with our attitude as we watch over souls. We must live with an awareness of our eventual need to give an account for them before God.

In 1 Peter 5:2 and 3 we read, "The elders which are among you I exhort...Feed the flock of God which is among you, taking the oversight, not by constraint, but willingly; not for filthy lucre, but of a ready mind; Neither as being lords over God's heritage, but being ensamples to the flock."

Taking oversight of the flock needs to be balanced with
•Feeding; not entertaining them and building a monument to my ministerial success.
•Not for money's sake; not taking a professional spiritual job, with my personal welfare in mind.
•With a ready mind; not a chore, because we know that is our lot in life and we do not want God to be mad at us.
•Not by constraint but willingly. We must minister because we love him who first loved us, and worship him with all we have and are. True ministry stems out of the continual flow of the springs of worship. When we have no true love and desire for the sheep and brethren, we need to stop. Get back to the cross and the blood shed for us. Rest, and enter into worship in the Spirit, and act out of the renewed relationship with God that will result.
•Taking oversight for all of the flock, and its needs, which is no small task. This means a balanced diet of food, ministry focus and the involvement of otherministries. This also includes considering their natural welfare, and directing their focus under God. We also need to address their protection from wrong unspiritual enemy strategies, as well as guiding them in matters of wrong. Quite a job. Thank God He gave us four more ministry callings to help us carry the load, as well as many others such as other elders, deacons, helps, governments, and more.
• Being an example to the flock. This is probably the most difficult area to fulfill under God. This requires a walk where we respond to others as the Lord Jesus would, since we are ambassadors in his stead (2 Cor. 5:20). He was and is Lord! Yet he never lorded over God's heritage. Instead he took a towel and told us to follow his example. "Ye call me Master and Lord: and ye say well; for so I am. If I then, your Lord and Master, have washed your feet; ye also ought to wash one another's feet (John 13: 13-14). *More towels and less self images are a spiritual prerequisite.*
More tough scriptures to follow:
•Matthew 20:28, "Even as the Son of man came not to be ministered unto, but to minister, and to give his life a ransom for many."
•1 Timothy 4:12, "Let no man despise thy youth; but be thou an example of the believers, in word, in conversation, in charity, in spirit, in faith, in purity."

124

•James 5:10 "Take, my brethren, the prophets, who have spoken in the name of the Lord, for an example of suffering affliction, and of patience."

These scriptures are impossible for us to comply with but for the grace of God. In a measure, by the help of the Holy Spirit, we can fulfill these to a degree. However, I thank God for Romans 8:1, and that I can claim there is no condemnation for me as I am in Christ Jesus and strive to walk after the Spirit. Without this knowledge I would be a total failure.

How we truly view ourselves in our own eyes in private says much about our application of the above scriptures. May we desire to see you as Lord, our Savior God, and not our own ministry image.

Authority and Responsibility

Let us focus on this other word which needs to be synonymous with authority, which is *responsibility*. One should never be given a place of authority under God, unless there is a dedication to responsibility for those under him. This responsibility should be visible, and depict the nature of God, as shown in the fruit of the Spirit (Gal. 5:22). This responsibility for the saints is Godward, as well as to the saints themselves. This should be visible in the ministry's direction, conduct, decisions, and communications.

A right spirit needs to accompany authority and responsibility. The spirit of this is shown in many scriptures, such as Acts 20:28. Paul stated to the elders over the church, "Take heed therefore unto yourselves, and to all the flock, over the which the Holy Ghost hath made you overseers, to feed the church of God, which he hath purchased with his own blood. The Holy Ghost had made them overseers and placed them in authority; however, this statement was cushioned with "take heed unto yourselves."

Be careful of how you carry and conduct yourself, as you take heed of the church (Acts 20:28). Bring an imbalance into your attitude, and you will no longer be properly taking care of the church. You will no longer be portraying accurately the heart and attitude of God the Father, Son, or Holy Spirit. Show a giant spirit of pride, as you walk in your God given authority, and you will destroy the purpose for which you were placed there. You will ultimately become one who in fact ministers destruction, as you destroy God in the minds of those you deal with. Just look at some churches *where those in authority name Christ, but no salvation goes forth.*

This text also says that the church is purchased by His own blood. The point is that the church is precious. God himself declares that, and if the SAINTS are not PRECIOUS in your sight, *get out of the ministry, as you are in a place of authority and ministering death!* You will be as a Pharisee who refuses to enter, and worse yet, you block the door to those who would. You portray another Christ who can not be perceived as the door. Your soul and spirit are on display. You are an epistle seen and read of all men (2 Cor. 3:2,3), and if you do not show the nature of Christ, they will see death as a portrayal of God, instead of life, love, and hope. Christ had much to say about people who do not portray Godly authority. "But woe unto you, Scribes and Pharisees, hypocrites! For ye shut up the kingdom of heaven against men: for ye neither go in yourselves, neither suffer ye them that are entering to go in" (Math 23:13).

The right spirit that needs to accompany authority is exemplified in Acts 20:31. Paul reminded them of the (true) tears that accompanied his ministry to them. In the same breath he spoke to them of the words of God's grace towards him and them. May we experience and remember this grace as we take a place of authority.

One powerful statement that says so much on this subject is 1 Thessalonians 2:7 and 8. "But we were gentle among you, even as a nurse cherisheth her children: So being affectionately desirous of you, we were willing to have imparted unto you, not the gospel of God only, but also our own souls, because ye were dear unto us." May we attain unto this. "Create in me a clean heart, Oh God, and renew a right spirit within me. Then shall I teach transgressors thy way, and sinners shall be converted unto thee" (Ps. 51:10,13).

Wrong Authority

Over the last couple of decades, *authority* has become a word to be feared in many places, due to the imbalances associated with this word. Some teachings on submission are totally unbalanced. This included a few who properly understood some teachings of five-fold ministry. They mistook their place under God and misrepresented true submission. Some taught their people that they could not make certain personal decisions unless they had the permission of those that were in authority. They missed a number of principles inherent in the word of God, including *the sovereign will of man.* They entered territory where they have no right. We in authority do not become God. God himself does not take authority in some matters, and leaves the choice to man. He allows man the right to make poor choices and face the results. This includes his choice for where he spends eternity (2 Pet. 3:9).

Have you ever considered that God does not always get HIS will, and refuses to impose it in certain situations? I said this to one ministry and he looked at me as if I had lost my mind.

God is holy. He created man in his image, and gave him a free will. in John 10:34 and 35, Jesus pointed out that they are called "gods" because the word of God came to them. He did not alter this stance, limit or disrespect man's free will, even when man was about to fall into sin in Eden.

In 2 Peter 3:9 and 1 Timothy 2:4, God expressly states that His will is that all men be saved. This is not going to happen, and to believe that everyone will be saved is to embrace the heretical doctrine of universalism. God sets men free to decide for Him or not, to seek or not to seek, to hunger for righteousness or not. God appeals to the heart of man to do the right and better thing, but allows him to express his will in any matter, including the most important one, salvation!

How much more should we act accordingly, and appeal to men's hearts to do the right, and not impose our will over them. Even if men follow the dictates of our will, we put them in bondage and under the law. To impose our will is to make us as God in their lives, and the wrong kind of god. We no longer reflect our true God. How can we dictate to someone to marry another person or not to marry? We can teach principles of godliness and conduct, but not pressure choices, even if we see a detrimental end.

We may see a forty year journey through the wilderness ahead for some as they exercise their right to make a wrong decision. We may see that the right decision will circumvent that journey and bring them to the promised land in a few days, but still must not take a wrong authority in their decision.

By all means use Godly wisdom, and act out your God-given responsibility. Counsel them as God counsels them. In Revelation 3:18 Jesus our Lord counsels us to buy from him gold tried in fire. Do not enter into areas where we have no right or abuse our position. *Until people are free from control over them, they are incapable of freely responding to God with their hearts.* An example is a young man who, because of his father's control and demands, attends church and fellowship activities. Let's see what he does when he is over eighteen, and free to make his own decisions with no peer pressure. The same person could be in submission to parents, and desire the things of God, and upon leaving home be faced with a whole new set of influences. He may respond for good or bad. We need to allow this setting free process in everyone's life.

Controls do not allow for the expression of free choice. If people rebel, it is between God and them. We have the privilege of interceding for them, and appealing to them for their good. God himself will deal with them. God does not have grandchildren. He will deal with children, similar to the spiritual father and the prodigal son. Even when it is painful, we are sometimes limited to praying and watching the horizon for their return.

My heart breaks for some saints, as I have seen abuse of authority. Some past friends joined a certain church group that took abusive and overt control over their people. We had been pillars in their lives, and poured the blessings of God into these people for several years. Then one day we saw changes, and observed them drawing away from us, and in time found out why. They were told to subtly draw away from all Christians who did not fellowship at their new church. We saw pain in many people due to this wrong teaching and control. These people were also told not to buy a home, or to sell their home without church leadership approval. The church authorities involved took complete control over their adherents. They told people to marry or not to marry. Cultish!

Years ago I met a Godly young woman, one of a number of Bible school students attached to a church in the Philippines. With a few other students and Godly young people, she was part of an island evangelism crusade and church planting team I ministered with. I heard she got married shortly after I left, and was somewhat surprised since I did not observe her showing any interest in the young man she married. Later I heard the entire story.

She married the young man because of pressure applied by the Godly, well meaning, but ignorant ministry in her life. The ministry saw a need for a follow up team to plant a church after our crusade, and imposed his will in this marriage, thinking that a couple would work better in ministry and follow up. Two years later, she fled from the young husband who had tried to stab her and chased her with a large knife. She managed to escape the island with her baby daughter, and was in the early stages of her second pregnancy. She moved far away to the city of Manila. Her life turned into an immoral mess, fed and pressured by poverty and the care of two children. Those who got her into this mess, whose wisdom she had trusted, only point a finger of accusation at her failures.

They played god in this situation. They should weep over their sin of presumptuous abuse of authority, and seek her out to help her in every way possible. A public apology to give understanding to the church and sow grace toward her would be in order. The young man fared no better. He was a zealous young Christian, and a first year Bible school student. Yes, there was a need to follow up the crusade, and we commend hearts of the elders in this point, but that did not justify abuse of authority.

In 1 Corinthians 7:36, it says, "Let them marry." Let them who choose to marry, marry within the guidelines that proceeded this statement. Let it be their choice, for their reasons. Not your choice and imposed decision due to your opinion of expediency. You step over the boundaries of your authority where you impose your will and manipulate circumstances.

This often is the case in a number of churches and ministries.

This even applies to the most important issue in peoples lives, salvation. There are denominations where most of the clergy put the fears and insecurities of their people to sleep. When humble and genuine inquirers express their unease and insecurities over their sure salvation, these clergy say, "Trust me, this is normal." They sentence their people to death. They play god in ignorance and presumption. They should tell these inquirers to seek the Lord in repentance, put their faith in the blood of Jesus and His love for them, until they find assurance of faith accompanied with joy.

Understand this principle. When people do something by law, and are not exercising their will, they are in bondage. The longer you encourage this state of bondage, the longer it will be before they can exercise their free will, and give themselves freely in all things to the Lord. Set them free! Do not manipulate or control. Appeal by presenting Godly love and principles. Encourage right decisions by teaching correct and Godly values. Let people decide for themselves. That is what God does! No one gets points in heaven by the works of the law, but by heart worship and free will offerings. If they make mistakes after you have carried out your responsibilities of teaching in a right spirit, let them. That is the only way that God can deal with them, and see the results He desires.

We learn by our mistakes. Do not interfere with a person's choices, unless it is to give Godly counsel, helping them see clearly in the process. God does not interfere. CONSIDER He sent Nathan the prophet to David after and not before David's failure.

Samuel told the people they were wrong to want a king like the other nations. He spoke the word of the Lord, not his own opinion. When the people demanded their way, God himself gave them King Saul. Knowing that they had sinned, and rejected God himself, God still did not depart from them and walk away angry. He gave them freedom to err. He still gave the best man available, and put a new heart in him after giving him some spiritual experience. Then when Saul failed, God did not say, "See I told you so, and now we are going back to the way things were before you demanded to have a king," but rather provided another king who turned out better. The people were allowed their choice, which eventually led them down hill. God allowed that and gave them THEIR choice, which eventually led to a nearly complete destruction of their relationship with Him! He teaches us the better way, and then stands back to let us make our decisions, knowing the end of the matter. That is God's wisdom, which is wiser and higher than ours. Teach us thy ways, Oh Lord!

Authority and Accountability

If you are going to stand in the place of authority, be Godly and accountable. There are those who demand that you submit to their authority, and they demand one way submission. You are to follow their directives without question. They see this as their god given placement and right. They do not know what God and spirit they are of (Lk. 9:55).

ONE WAY SUBMISSION IS A SPIRIT OF CONTROL. Anyone who displays this posture, under a religious guise of spirituality, is of a wrong spirit. There are authorities in the body, and we need to understand how we are to submit to them; they are to understand how to exercise the complete laws of submission.

I will never again submit myself to any man unless it is with the understanding of MUTUAL ACCOUNTABILITY. I will submit to all with this understanding in place. I submit to you. You be accountable to me. Take the time and be assessable answer any "Why?" I am not a mushroom to be kept in the dark. Give me understanding. Do not ask me to follow blindly. God does not ask that of me. Like Paul, teach me the whole counsel of God (Acts 20). Be transparent. In this relationship I promise to honor, uphold, love and submit myself to you, and be accountable in word and action.

Consider Ephesians 5:20 to 22. "In the name of our Lord Jesus Christ; Submitting yourselves one to another in the fear of God. Wives, submit yourselves unto your own husbands, as unto the Lord." Verse 22 does not delete the contents of verse 21. This may jar some male egos, and that is my prayer. One text theology is usually biased and incorrect, so let's consider one more.

"Likewise, ye younger, submit yourselves unto the elder.

Yea, all of you be subject one to another, and be clothed with humility: for God resisteth the proud, and giveth grace to the humble" (1 Pet. 5:5). Submitting yourselves one to another applies right along with wives submit yourselves to your husbands. You younger submit to the elder applies right along with all of you submit one to another. THIS WAS SAID TO THE ELDERS, as well as to the younger. Read the preceding context. One who resists this is resisted by God himself because of his pride (verse 5).

If Peter and John had defied authority and obeyed God rather than men, the church and the cause of Christ would have suffered (Acts 4:19). Sometimes we deny so-called authority when it differs from God's authority. If Nabal had listened to his wife Abigail, his life and eternity would have been different (1 Sam. 25:14). Dealing with people without reason is ungodly. We become their conscience, and sin by becoming god in their lives. We need to be accountable, hear, and reason with our fellow man. "But sanctify the Lord God in your hearts: and be ready always to give an answer to every man that asks you a reason of the hope that is in you with meekness and fear" (1 Pet. 3:15). If we are to have a reason for any man, how much more should we give a reason to the church of Jesus Christ.

If this were not so, a wife would have to listen and obey her husband when he ordered her to break the law. No! We in authority need to be willing to submit to the least of God's saints. We know our place of authority, and they should know our authority as well. May we learn to follow only Godly authority, with Holy liberty. Teach us your ways, our Lord and God. By your grace grant us a right understanding. May we, like Solomon, be given wisdom and understanding to govern the affairs of the church and your people. Grant us a right spirit, Lord.

Chapter 11

FIVE-FOLD ELDERSHIP AUTHORITY, AND SCRIPTURAL BASIS

Authority and Submission

In Hebrews 13:17, Paul says to the church, "Obey them that have the rule over you, and submit yourselves: for they watch for your souls, as they that must give account [to God]."

Ministers and elders should remember that we will give an account to God. As we look back at all those we had to deal with, few would not wince at the memory or not be convicted of failure. I do. Nevertheless, despite our failures, God uses imperfect vessels to do his perfect will.

Few in the church deny the necessity of submission to eldership, or require teaching on the subject. Many in eldership require teaching on submission to eldership, and deny the scriptural teachingof it in deed if not in word. More than that, many need to apply "all of you submit yourselves one to another." We need to be accountable to those who submit to us. Should a two-week-old babe in Christ point out failure in our lives, may we have the humility to listen and be corrected. I hope the babe would do so in a gentle spirit, as we would with them, because it would be so much easier to receive correction.

I will never forget the young Christian who overheard my negative statements and opinions on a certain fast music gospel musician. He made me accountable for my words, and informed me that he got saved due to the music ministry of that very musician. I repented, being totally convicted about my words. I asked him to forgive me, telling him I would not voice that opinion again. That conversation changed my opinion. We still have a quality relationship today. Had I displayed a different attitude, this would not have been the case. Be accountable.

In 1 Corinthians 16:15 and 16, Paul says, "I beseech you, brethren, ye know the house of Stephanas, that it is the first fruits of Achaia , and that they have addicted themselves to the ministry of the saints, That ye submit yourselves unto such, and to every one that helpeth with us, and laboureth." We see here an admonishment for us to observe and appreciate those who are in ministry.

No problem. However, we are also told to submit ourselves to such. *A definite problem.* Recently I talked to a ministry about the insincerity of his words. He had said five times over a two year period, "We just have to get together for coffee."" Every time I left him I said, "I am ready when you are. Call me." He said he would, but never did, and I did not want to hear this a sixth time. I was also hoping that my conversation might jar him into a genuine offer to attempt to build a bridge.

During conversation in the privacy of his office, he informed me he did not remember his statements, and in actuality he did not really even know me. He was affronted. I left him rather sad, thinking about the end of this conversation and how often this happens among ministries at large. Empty words, not knowing those that labor in the same vineyard, and in reality not wanting to know them.

In Acts 20:17 and 28, all the elders were overseers to the flock, told to take heed of the sheep and feed them. Scriptural leadership is a plurality leadership with the elders submitting one to another.

Scriptural Authority

This is where the going gets a little tough. This is where you are challenged to let go of traditions, church practices, and the opinions you have come to over the years. This is where you are challenged to drop all thinking on this subject except that which the New Testament portrays. If you accept that the church today does not have to measure up to the first century church, read no further. You are wasting your time and this is not for you! For those who are of a different mind, let's continue. Elisha had to press on to get the double portion.

As stated in previous chapters, we find five ministries given as gifts to the church in Ephesians 4:11. The authority flow of those ministries is portrayed in 1 Corinthians 12:17-28. "If the whole body were an eye, where were the hearing If the whole were hearing, where were the smelling? But now hath God set the members every one of them in the body, as it hath pleased him. Now ye are the body of Christ, and members in particular. And God hath set some in the church, first apostles, secondarily prophets, thirdly teachers, after that miracles, then gifts of Healings, helps, governments, diversities of tongues."

First, secondarily, third, after that and then. These are Greek original words translated into English from God's holy word. Unfortunately, these words are read over with no significance placed on them. In 99.9% of churches, no sermon is ever preached on these words. This is due to change! There is an authority order under the God of order in the church. Only man's ignorance— and willful ignorance—will ignore and deny this order. How terrible that the most precious thing in all the earth, the church of Jesus Christ, has ignored the structuring of God. We have not listened, nor spent quality time trying to understand and apply these words. Lord, I repent.

Apostles First

Why? Simply because God's Word says so. Do not allow for that "Saul spirit." Remember that obedience is better than sacrifice.

We can not understand the answer to this question unless we understand the make up of an apostle. A God-ordered and ordained apostle has unique strengths and qualities. This calling comes with a Holy Ghost equipping. You do not grow into this or any other calling, unless you are called to it. The Apostle has a world vision. If his hands are upheld, he will establish the gospel in new territory until all the earth is reached. In maturity he will raise up and direct growing ministries, be a defender of sound doctrine, direct the affairs of several churches, have a miracle ministry, and operate in several gifts of the Spirit. He will probably function with an anointing for impartation with the laying on of hands. He has a special burden for other ministries, and wants to see them excel and function. He has a commander's view of the battle, and the eye of the Lord to set the battle array.

The difficult part is to identify the Apostle. It may even be more difficult to receive him, since we may have preconceived ideas of what he should look like. He may be ill-clad and working with his hands. He may be crippled and beat up, since he has had nothing but rejection until now. Be sure of this, there are a number of them in the body of Christ. I know at least ten of them, here and overseas, and some need major healing, loving, and balancing. Understanding themselves and why they are different from other ministries brings some healing. BEING RECEIVED IN THEIR CALLING BRINGS MUCH MORE. When we do, be prepared to receive an apostle's reward (Math. 10:41). We will not receive the reward until we receive the apostle. People did not receive from Jesus until they received him (Mk. 6:5). Think about it. May those honored by this calling mature and establish the Kingdom of God. I see some apostles with that burden and vision that are evangelicals, not understanding the baptism of the Holy Spirit. One evangelical apostle I know is pastoring with a vision to raise up ministries and send them out. A pastor may grow in his understanding and vision for the need of missions, but an apostle lives and breaths this vision even if no man ever portrayed it to him. This is because of his God-given equipping that comes with the calling.

Prophets Second

The prophet flows in the wind of the Spirit and frequents high and lofty heights with God. He is the eyes of fire to the church, and brings holiness to God's people. He operates in the revelation gifts, as well as the power gifts of the Holy Spirit. Make room and receive God's prophets and prophetesses. They are the second authority in the church, and often God's spokesmen. Receive them, and you will receive their reward. There are many of them, and they are named along with apostles as foundation ministries (Eph. 2:20). Many are wounded, due to rejection. For some this is self imposed; they sometimes get into the "Moses syndrome," sometimes identifying with God more than man. When this happens, as one pointed out to me recently, they end up as the "prophet in a cave."

Cave-dwelling prophets still function in their gift ministry, but do not flow with a church body. They will be like Moses when he had completed his visit with God on the mountain. Seeing the sin in the people, they become critical and not identify with them. They forget that "all have sinned and come short of the glory of God." This is evidenced by a lack of gentle long suffering and by subtle pride in their revelation knowledge and spiritual gifting. The result is a "super spiritual" and critical attitude. In this case, they are likely to experience God's special love for them in causing them to hew stone slabs, to carry up mountains. This reminds any of us as to where the power, anointing and gifting comes from. When they remember the source of their gifting and anointing, they will be used greatly.

I remember one person who portrayed herself as a ministry. She pointed at a victim with a long outstretched finger, and in a shrill voice demanded, "Do you receive what the prophet said?" Even if the word given had some revelation truth, this carnal action destroyed the word and ministered death to the recipient. The Spirit of the Lord is gentle, and an elder must be gentle as well.

When God deals with a person who has a wrong spirit, like Moses (a prophet), they will in that hour intercede for the people with a changed heart (Num. 14:12). A truly mature prophet will flow with a segment of the body of Christ, and should be honored and received according to the placement given under God.

Prophets are blessed with awesome gifts, but they must also develop an elder's caring heart, and if you will, pastoral abilities. To deny and resist their placement is to deny Christ, His structure, and His true Lordship over His body.

Prophets are placed in an authoritative role in the body of Christ. If we simply accept the word of God on this as stated in 1 Corinthians 12:28, we lose half our mental struggles. How do we work out functional relationships with the other ministries, as the prophet comes in and goes out? The prophet ministry, who so badly needs to be received in the church, sadly may be the last ministry to ultimately flow with the Lord's given authority pattern. This is due to their powerful foundation ministry gifting. May they see the word and wisdom of God in the directive to flow in submission to and with apostolic authority.

The home eldership team needs to be very flexible to have liberty to flow under Holy Spirit unction. If we work out a Godly, sensitive, edifying relationship, the angels in heaven will rejoice and our Lord will be glorified. We will all be blessed when the prophet ministering by revelation, word exposition, and spiritual gifts.

Teachers Third

Immediately some will say, "What about the pastors?" I have been asked this question many times. May we get a revelation of this one simple truth. 1 Samuel 15:22 tells us that "obedience is better than sacrifice" when Samuel confronted the Saul spirit. In this authority placement the word of God is clear, whether we understand it or not. Ours is to obey.

Teachers are those who have a greater focus on imparting truth than addressing other care needs of the flock. May we give them their God given place among elders, knowing and being aware that the Lord Jesus Christ himself placed them as described in 1 Corinthians 12:28. God's people perish due to lack of knowledge. Pastors impart knowledge as well, just like all ministries, but their message is more often inspirational. The teacher establishes knowledge of doctrine, line upon line, and precept upon precept. May they be received and grow as they are allowed to exercise their calling and ministry.

Chain of Command?

Does this mean that if the apostle, prophet or teacher has an opinion or direction while dealing with the affairs of the body of Christ, that we always listen to this order of opinion no matter what? Of course not. This was not to be a regimented, legalistic approach to government, and "all of you be submissive one to an other" still applies. May we give place in our hearts to the principal of this authority, and be aware this is the placement of the Lord Jesus himself. Those blessed with these callings have feet of clay and are still human beings and error prone (Gal. 2:11). May we recognize their placement by the decision and wisdom of God himself. May we consider the third authority ministry in our decision processes, as we direct the affairs of the church, and allow God's government to flow as he designed.

When we will do this, we will be blessed. It will take grace and humility to see this authority become reality, and see this flow in functional unity. To do this is to trust in the Lord and his word. To reject it is to deny God's wisdom and authority in our lives, and claim we are wiser than God. Deny this, and deny your right to ever again demand your place of authority, or speak on the subject of authority. If you yourself refuse God's rightful authority, you will be speaking in hypocrisy.

Pastors and Evangelists

We have no scriptural exactness about who is of a higher authority between these callings. We do know they are part of the called five-fold ministry in Ephesians 4:11, as much as the other ministries, and as necessary for the balanced growth of the church.

We also know that pastors are not to be the ministry heads of churches. Most churches today are under pastor's authority. This is not meant as less than total respect for pastors. Thank you, Lord, for every one of these brethren, and sisters in some cases. Pastors still need to submit to the word of God, and make room for the God-outlined structure in the New Testament. If you really preach faith, I challenge you to exercise some in this major matter, and trust God for the results. In Luke 1:52, Mary, blessed of God and under the anointing, said that God exalts those of low degree.

Some will no doubt try to hide behind the smoke screen of, "I am submissive to the leadership of my denomination." Sorry, that will not hold water. That would be denying and avoiding your responsibility under God. We are to walk by his word. After all, is this not what we preach to our people continuously? Is Jesus your Lord? Is an organization larger than Him? Do you see the need to be part of an apostolic structure and headship today? A number of ministries called pastors might really be some other calling. In any case, it is presumptuous and sinful to knowingly call yourself something you are not. All pastors and evangelists should be part of a multiple leadership structure. All should know their proper callings, and all understand a proper authority order, including the foundation ministries.

Respect those who are in your ministry structure, as the Lord wants you to. Until you are part of what you in your heart know to be apostle-led multiple elder leadership, you have come short of and frustrated the hand of God. You are out of order. Think about it. The book of Acts will continue in its fullness, when this structure is correct and accepted again.

Scriptural Example of Apostles' Authority and Submission

We find that the scriptural values and the admonishment of 1 Peter 5:5 were exemplified throughout the Holy New Testament. "All of you be submissive one to another." Scriptures illuminate one another, and never transgress or set another scripture at naught. So we see in Acts 8:14, where the apostles at Jerusalem sent a submissive Peter and John. Again, we see the same thing in Acts 11:22, where the apostle Barnabas was sent out to perform a ministry task.

We then observe the apostles Barnabas and Paul accepting Holy Ghost direction and submitting to the ministry of the other elders in Antioch (Acts 13:1-3). The eldership, made up of teachers, prophets, and more, laid hands on them and sent them out.

We see the real picture of apostles submitting to not just apostles, but to the apostles and elders in Jerusalem (Acts 15:2). They did not take the position of "we are apostles and the highest authority and we say this is the way it is." They submitted a question of doctrine to the multitude of counsel of the multiple Jerusalem eldership. They recognized the maturity and strength of the Jerusalem apostle-led ministry. They did not take the question to the Antioch eldership which sent them out. They understood the apostles doctrine of Acts 2:42, but also recognized the elders with the apostles.

In chapter 15:27, we find the *apostles sending out prophets* for a specific task, and the prophets fulfilling this task in submission to the apostles. When apostles are given their rightful God intended place, the multiple ministry will flow, and the church will be blessed with a banquet table. A key reason is that a truly called apostle will have a father's heart for the church. Paul said in 1 Corinthians 4:15, "You may have many instructors, (ministries) but few fathers." I remember distinctly when I, as an apostle, was busy ministering to churches overseas. Several times someone said, "You really have a father's heart." Each time I controlled my emotions, but get weepy inside, thinking, "That is my heart towards these churches and people. " Finding this text helped me understand myself.

The same text also depicts Paul telling the church that he might come with a rod or a spirit of meekness. In my life and ministry, I have flowed under the love of God for his people on numerous occasions. However, on several occasions I have also seen people die in judgment, and that within one day of the spoken word. Many others could also tell of similar dealings under God.

We see the authority of these apostles accepted and recognized by the churches they ministered to. In Acts 14:27, Paul and Barnabas gathered the church of Antioch on their arrival. It does not say they reported in to the local elders, and the local eldership decided to gather the church. No doubt the elders cooperated in this effort, but clearly the gathering was set in array by the two apostles. I also believe the elders were thrilled to be part of the whole thing, with no bad attitudes. As in 1 Corinthians 16:1, Paul gave orders to churches, and they submitted to these orders as unto the Lord.

In my life and ministry, I have seen pain and devastation caused when others have corrupted their authority place because of ignorance or empire vision. In the late eighties, I took a ministry team on a Holy Ghost-inspired assignment. We held a tremendous crusade in the northwestern Philippines, where the crowd doubled every night. Because of the many miracles, people still came out of the mountains six weeks after we were gone, asking about "the people that prayed." Sister Susan Quan, who is a gifted interpreter, and ministers in a Bible school in San Fernando, blessed us with her ministry. This resulted in a church explosion under a certain national ministry, who was gifted and called and anointed of God.

As time went by, a prophetess ministry, blessed of God and whom I had encouraged in Philippine ministry, visited this group of growing churches, and took teams there. At the time I was buried in personal problems and did not visit for an eighteen month period. This prophetess reasoned that the Lord had given her the oversight of the work. The problem arose when the key ministry ran into spiritual problems. I lost my voice because of that and could not correct the ministry involved. That ministry may not have heard me anyway, but the lack of support was a key element in the breaking. My discernment of the situation was quite different than hers. Eventually I separated myself from that whole gospel explosion, as my authority was taken away and undermined by one who did not uphold and recognize scriptural authority. She said, "God has joined my heart to that ministry." Praise God for a mutual appreciation for the other ministry, but the damage resulting from her stance was incalculable, and the results are evident today. I have chosen to separate myself from such. I could not build a trusting relationship with one such as this, until her understanding was correct, though I still love the people involved.

We also see where Paul advised a church to receive his fellow apostle, Barnabas, whom he had sent. Barnabas under God flowed with this authority. He went, and the church received.

Apostle's Authority Delegated and Received

The apostle often sets things in order. This was part of their care of all the churches (2 Cor. 11:28). For example, in 1 Corinthians 11:34, Paul said he would set things in order when he visited Corinth, referring to issues regarding Christian conduct. In Philippians 1:1 we see him directing a letter to the saints, elder/bishops, and deacons. His letter was a directive on how they should live before God and conduct themselves.

In 1 Thessalonians 3:5 and 6 we see Paul sending Timothy, who went at his directive, respecting the senior apostle. We also see him commanding the prophet Silas and Timothy to come to meet with him with all speed (Acts 17:15). In chapter 19:22, he sent Erastus and Timothy. Then in Acts 20:17, he sent for the plural elders of Ephesus, who came at his request. Clearly the apostle was governing the church work, sending and directing ministry traffic. It is a powerful demonstration of those who received these commandments and directions, as unto the Lord.

How do you feel about this? Could this happen today? Would you allow the Lord to use someone in your life as portrayed in Acts? What would the results be?

The churches and ministries affected by this God given and Christ centered scriptural ministry authority and flow will see a tremendous blessing of balance and anointing. We will see the accounts of Acts and the results demonstrated in our day. Other scriptures that portray this, such as 1 Timothy 1:1,2, and 3; Titus 1:5; and Titus 3:12 and 13. Here Titus was given the authority to ordain issues in churches.

Apostle's Soft Authority

Without a correct spiritual attitude, no authority will flow and include a holy regard for all involved. The authority examples given in the New Testament demonstrate the correct attitude of the ministry submitted to Jesus Christ. They show a spirit of love and respect for their fellow ministry. When Paul wanted the teacher Apollos to come to Corinth, he allowed room in his thinking for Apollos to go there as he felt led in God's time. Later we find that Apollos came, as Paul requested him to. They both showed respect and cooperation, yet were an example of respect for authority. May it be.

We see a gem of an example in 2 Corinthians 10:1, where Paul eloquently says to the church, "I beseech you in the meekness and gentleness of Christ." If this spirit was exemplified in emerging apostles, prophets, and teachers today, Christ's authority structure would be received much more readily. We read in chapter 10:8, "For though I should boast somewhat of our authority which the Lord has given us, it is for edification and not destruction." He gently says to Timothy in 1 Timothy 1:1 and 2, "Paul [dad] to my son in the faith."

May apostles and prophets who are involved with encouraging and directing other growing ministries demonstrate this love and gentleness to all, and thereby demonstrate the heart of Christ.

Apostle and Ministry Authority Attitude

2 Corinthians 10:12, "For we dare not make ourselves of the number, or compare ourselves with some that commend themselves: but they measuring themselves by themselves, and comparing themselves among themselves, are not wise."
This is applicable then and now. So often, being flesh and blood, we are tempted to measure ourselves against others. I am as good as so and so. I am better than so and so. So and so thinks well of me and gives me their approval. Seventeen people said I preached a great message. We tend to desire the approval of men, when we should be looking for the approval of God. May we desire your approval only, oh Lord. May we glory in you alone (2 Cor. 10:17). Paul knew he did not come one whit behind any other ministry or apostle , and still demonstrated this attitude (2 Cor. 11:5).

A profound attitude is expressed in Galatians 3:5. Here Paul says, "holy apostles and prophets." We find the same statement made in heaven in Revelation 18:20. We do well to consider this. May we consider our fellow ministry with this understanding. May we see this attitude of holy brethren applied today. May we see the end of the empire vision, of I am of Paul or Apollos, and you are my competition (Eph. 3:5). May we remember we are made ministers by the grace of God, and our ministry makes God the Father, Son, and Holy Ghost somebody (Eph. 3:7).

We are admonished to submit to every one that labors in the Lord (1 Cor. 16:16). All submission within the body of Christ is meant to be Christ-like, and as unto the Lord. Where anyone demands submission in an un- Christ-like spirit, address them about this issue. It is sin! Wherever we shrink from submission in a right spirit and a Godly manner, may we repent, and desire change. If so, God will bless, since he exalts men of low degree.

May we serve him with all of our hearts, and worship him, for he is worthy of all glory honor and power. We love you, Lord,

Chapter 12

AUTHORITY AND JUDGMENT IN THE BODY OF CHRIST; RESPONSIBILITY

Judgment

"Judge not, that ye be not judged" (Math. 7:1). This is the first and last statement on the topic of judgment that you will hear from the world, or at your local bar. Unfortunately, this is also true of many in the church. They have not considered or are not aware of other scriptures dealing with this subject, such as 1 Corinthians 5:12 and 13. "For what have I to do to judge them also that are without? Do not ye judge them that are within? But them that are without God judgeth." Therefore put away from among yourselves that wicked person.

Judge not, and judge!

No, these scriptures do not contradict each other. We simply need to learn what we are to judge, and what we are to leave alone. We need to have a clear distinction between those who are within and those who are without. Our Lord Jesus did and does, as expressed in his prayer of John chapter seventeen.

First of all, we are not to judge those who are without, meaning those not of the church and citizens of God's Kingdom. God will judge them. Truly spiritual people discern between saved and unsaved people, and this has nothing to do with church membership. If we applied this knowledge, we would see many more brought to the Kingdom. Some destroy their ability to witness and love others to Christ, because they criticize unbelievers and their ways and habits

We are to be epistles and examples seen and read of all men, and understand that they can not see or enter the kingdom of God until they are born again (Jn. 3:3,5). Their spiritual blindness is taken away when they come to Christ (2 Cor. 3:14,15). So let's not judge them, but lead them to Christ. Then the Holy Ghost will deal with sanctification and cleansing. What good does it do them if they quit smoking or drinking or reading pornography, as long as they are still headed for hell? Get them saved! Usually, they are aware of their sin. When a ministry is preaching to the lost, this rule changes. Then we are duty bound to preach sin, hell and eternal judgment, and leave the results to God. May we have a Godly wisdom in dealing with the lost.

Secondly, we are to judge those that are within, but we need to be aware of what the limits of judgment are. According to 1 Corinthians 5:12, we are to judge sin in the body of Christ, and only things involving right and wrong and sin. This includes debate and wrong between brethren. This judgment and confrontation is distinct from discerning right from wrong in all people and situations.

1 Corinthians 6:1 to 5, "Dare any of you, having a matter against another, go to law before the unjust, and not before the saints? 2 Do ye not know that the saints shall judge the world? and if the world shall be judged by you, are ye unworthy to judge the smallest matters? Know ye not that we shall judge angels? how much more things that pertain to this life? If then ye have judgments of things pertaining to this life, set them to judge who are least esteemed in the church. I speak to your shame."

It is clear the church is to judge matters of dispute in the family of God, and it is to our shame when we do not do so, knowing we will ultimately be judging angels. Jesus himself taught that the highest court of judgment was the church. In disputes of sin and wrong, we are to avail ourselves of the judgment court of the church.

"Take it to the church" (Math. 18:17). Yes, those are the words of the Lord of the church. When there is debate, strife and sin and you cannot resolve the matter personally or with two or three others, take the offending person to the church. The church must judge the matter. This judgment has power, so it must be correct and righteous. If the church's judgment is not followed, the impenitent person is treated as a heathen and a publican. This is the direction given by the Lord Jesus Christ himself to those who are wrong!

A church without a multiple eldership and a multiple care ministry *is incapable of flowing with the God-given directives on this subject.* It takes a mature multiple leadership to carry out this task. As a matter of fact, a church without a multiple eldership, meaning a plurality of spiritually mature leadership, will be deficient in it's ability to minister fully to all the needs of their people. The comparison would be Moses judging Israel before his father-in-law corrected him. In response to this correction Moses chose seventy elders to deal with matters (Exod. 18:13-26). We are also robbed of the wisdom of the multitude of counsel. "Where no counsel is, the people fall: but in the multitude of counselors there is safety" (Prov. 11:14).

People are falling because they lack a multitude of counselors. Many ministries do not want to get their hands dirty with the dirty problems in peoples' lives. More often the problem comes down to covetousness over finances. If the controlling ministry has a wrong understanding in this area, he will limit the multitude of ministry, eldership, and counselors to protect his financial corner.

Even more often the real problem is that the person in charge does not want to share his authority throne. As a result only a limited number of things can be addressed, since the poor overworked ministry is only one man and can do only so much. Perhaps the person who breaks under the overload of ministry is allowed to do so because they are taking on a task God never gave them to carry. The load is to be distributed to a multiple eldership. There will not be adequate room for judgment in the body of Christ and the local church until the structure is corrected. Until this correction has been made, the unspoken sign in the window is court closed. It is interesting to note there were elders in Israel prior to Moses appointing the seventy. Like today, *they were benched and ignored.* Moses also ran into an overload experience, and by the wisdom of God appointed seventy elders to share the ministry load. Unlike today, they did not vote them out after they got two years experience.

While officiating at a wedding recently, I spoke to a mature man who is my namesake. He had been a Christian for over twelve years and an elder in training for several years. He attended a church where a number of people had been in the same position over the years, but few ever attain and graduate. Although I hid my knowledge and perceptions, it tore my heart as this person shared how God anointed his trip and ministry as he visited his country of origin. He had exciting things to share about ministry outside of his home church. The absence of an equal report within his home church was stifling and spoke of the bondage imposed on him by the one (I know) who consistently usurps authority at the top. **Hear, oh Israel, set my people free.**

Third, there are many things we are not to judge. Jesus warned against wrong judgment in Matthew 7:1. The wrong judgment was about a mote, or speck in our brother's eye. If there is to be any judgment, limit it to a brother. This does not mean we do not discern sin and wrong in the world and shun it. However, we do not criticize the unbeliever. Chances are they know their sin. In any case, I have not seen an unbeliever come to Christ due to being criticized. I have won them through loving and not criticizing. Wait for the moment when they will open up for you to speak, and gently lead them to Christ.

When judging a brother, be sure that it is more than a speck you want to address in his eye. Remember that you will be judged by the standards that you set for others, now and in eternity. Consider our own beam-sized problems as we are tempted to judge. "For with what judgment ye judge, ye shall be judged: and with what measure ye mete, it shall be measured to you again. And why beholdest thou the mote that is in thy brother's eye, but considerest not the beam that is in thine own eye?" (Math. 7:2,3)

Many things are simply a critical spirit, operating in the ministry of criticism. A critical spirit is a wrong spirit. Consider Romans 14. I have, and was convicted to repent as I did. In verses one to three, Paul discusses our beliefs about eating meat, or being a vegetarian, and tells us that we are not to judge or criticize the person who believes differently than ourselves in this matter. He then points out that if we judge anyone according to this matter, we are judging an other man's servant, namely God's servant. I eat meat. I am not to judge or be critical of a Seventh Day Adventist, who does not. They may be weak in the faith, and destroyed by my debate over this matter.

More important areas of discussion are the deity of Christ, the new birth, and the doctrine of substitutionary atonement. I have debated with these people from time to time over Sabbath teachings and other doctrines that came up when I was dealing with some who came out of these churches. The shrimp and meat questions always comes up. This is a subject that I am not to debate with them. In verse six, it says that he who eateth not, to the Lord he eateth not, and giveth God thanks. Rather, help them to understand we are saved by grace through faith, and not works of the law. Perhaps point them to Romans chapter fourteen, and show them they are not to judge you as you partake of some foods as unto the Lord.

Romans 14:8 to 10 tells us whether we are alive or dead, we are the Lord's. Why then do we judge a brother and set him at naught? How many sinful critical judgments and comments have been made about clothing, food, hairdos, personal habits and tastes that have upset brothers and sisters in the Lord? How about criticism over someone else's financial giving, when all of this is their personal worship unto the Lord, who will judge in this life and the next, and reward accordingly. Verse 15 speaks about us grieving a brother about meat and wine, and thereby walking in an unloving manner, and destroying the person Christ died for. For these things it is written, why dost thou judge thy brother?

We may exhort, encourage, and pray, and discern when to apply each of these, but we should not judge or be critical in attitude over many things, *except sin, where we must judge.*

God Loves Judgment

Our God says that He changes not. Praise God! Otherwise there would be no foundation to our faith in salvation. He is the Lord. Holy and Righteous is His name. He constantly judges and searches the hearts of men.

In Jeremiah 17:10, God said, "I the Lord search the hearts."

"For the eyes of the LORD run to and fro throughout the whole earth, to show himself strong in the behalf of them whose heart is perfect toward him" (2 Chr. 16:9).

"I the Lord love judgment" (Isai. 61:8).

The queen of Sheba made a tremendous royal statement in 1 Kings 10:9. "Blessed be the Lord thy God, which delighted in thee, to set thee on the throne of Israel: because the LORD loved Israel for ever, therefore made he thee king, to do judgment and justice."

The Holy Ghost made us elders, to do judgment and justice. This lady had insight. God loved Israel enough to provide a King who would practice judgment and justice. DO WE BELIEVE THAT GOD LOVES THE CHURCH ENOUGH TO PROVIDE ELDERS WHO PRACTICE JUDGMENT AND JUSTICE? May we become wise men and consider Solomon, who was triple blessed of God for his correct request. He asked for understanding to discern judgment, with a wise and understanding heart (1 Kings 3:11).

We read in Psalm 37:28, "For the LORD loveth judgment, and forsaketh not his saints; they are preserved for ever: but the seed of the wicked shall be cut off." May we not forsake the saints, and carry out the will of God as faithful stewards and servants. We are wicked if we forsake Holy judgment.

Lastly, we find this awesome verse, "Run ye to and fro through the streets of Jerusalem, and see now, and know, and seek in the broad places thereof, if ye can find a man, if there be any that executeth judgment, that seeketh the truth; and I will pardon it" (Jer. 5:1).

May we be of those whom the Lord will see executing judgment. We who are the heavenly Jerusalem (Heb. 12:22) and minister to those who have come to the heavenly Jerusalem will bring unfathomable blessing to the church. May we be the priesthood who before God will execute judgment. May we seek out truth and avert God's need to deal in judgment (1 Cor. 11:30,31). May we bring in a harvest of God's mercy and pardon.

One of the most painful things in my life occurred when an overseas ministry with a place of authority fell into wrong ways. This affected another ministry. This second ministry purchased a motorcycle from the one fallen into wrong ways. He paid cash for it and donated it for gospel usage. This ministry had to pay for it a second time when creditors came presented their claims for payment of the original acquisition, repairs, and modifications. The ministry in error who sold the motorcycle was confronted and refused to be accountable. The real pain came when another State-side ministry, not wanting to hear any evil, upheld this wayward ministry, not willing to deal with the matter. The affect in part was the undermining of my voice in this matter, rather than supporting me. This painfully affected my authority and relationship with those involved, and ultimately affected a number of churches and outreaches, and hurt several ministries. The wrong values and judgment in this matter cost Christ and the Kingdom of God, as well as pain to my heart and others. We must judge those within. May the Lord turn these circumstances.

Judgment By and In the Church

1 Corinthians 6:2 to 4, "Do ye not know that the saints shall judge the world? and if the world shall be judged by you, are ye unworthy to judge the smallest matters? Know ye not that we shall judge angels? how much more things that pertain to this life? If then ye have judgments of things pertaining to this life, set them to judge who are least esteemed in the church."

God requires that we fulfill this word. People need to know the welcome mat is out for dealing with their struggles and problems between each other. They need to know we desire to uphold them. This means carefully, lovingly, and in a sensitive manner allowing them the comfort of airing difficulties. This will greatly eliminate struggles, gossip, and relationship problems, provided that issues are addressed candidly, and with a gentle, reconciliatory spirit.

Pharisees were accused by our elder brother, Jesus, of laying heavy burdens on people and not lifting one finger to help them (Math. 23:4). May we avoid appearances of similarities. It is impossible, especially in larger churches, for proper and gracious judgment to be enacted, unless there is a multiple and functional ministry eldership in place.

In my recent life I wound up with a difference between a brother and myself over a business matter. The brother refused to talk to me and others whom I had asked to communicate with him at my request. I asked a local pastor to approach the pastor of the church where this person attended to arrange a meeting to deal with this issue. This pastor who had the largest growing local church refused to deal with this matter, saying, "How do I know this person [meaning me] is even saved?"

The results of his failure to act was that the brother involved unrighteously dealt with the matter through worldly unsaved lawyers. Since we both knew a number of Christian people, who somehow came to hear of these events, this affected a number of relationships, and some adversely. All of these people no doubt heard parts and pieces about it from the church gossip trail. This church gossip trail exists and thrives because the pastor and leadership refused to search out and judge the matter. Ultimately, they are responsible for the separations between friends and acquaintances, and death caused along the gossip trail. A proper ministry structure averts this problem if they address their responsibilities.

The most painful part of this dilemma was the affect on children and family of the brother involved. My wife and I had a great desire to bless this person, and be a witness to his children and unsaved family through the intended blessing. The pastor and leadership who refused to deal with this matter are responsible for the death that occurred in this person's family. There was also death within the brother and his wife, bitterness, strife and the negative results of unresolved issues. All of this would have been laid at rest through righteous judgment. The ministry who refused this request for church judgment will bear the harvest of his decision.

In 1 Timothy 5:19, we read, "Against an elder receive not an accusation, but before two or three witnesses." We are told that two or three witnesses need to be present before we allow ourselves to hear an accusation against an elder. This is not meant to be a rule to enlarge gossip. The others are called witnesses because the one making the accusation will be judged for his or her words. Any accusation of an elder must be addressed and judged. In other words, if someone makes a negative comment against an elder, they should always be prepared to give an account of themselves and their conversation. No one should hear the accusation without taking the Godly responsibility of bringing the matter before the church elders, so they can judge the contents of the accusation. If we are going to obey the word of God, we should apply this, and when we do, it might have an impact on our churches, on both eldership and people. All will be held accountable. Holiness and peace, and maybe even unity will result. HALLELUJAH !

Judgment In Church is Essential

"Ye who turn judgment to wormwood, and leave off righteousness in the earth" (Amos 5:7). *"But let judgment run down as waters, and righteousness as a mighty stream"* (Amos 5:24).

The ministry eldership of the flock are to be guardians and watchmen, especially of Bible and doctrinal truths. There is only one gospel, summarized by salvation through faith in Jesus Christ, our Lord and Savior. Many groups and cults portray another doctrine. Most of them appeal to works, including church sacraments like infant baptism, or the giving of money. Some project another Christ, although in truth there is no other Christ. They deny the doctrine of the deity of Christ. They do not agree with Isaiah 9:6, where we are taught that the Son that was given is also the Everlasting Father. We must judge, and draw a line between acceptable and unacceptable teaching within the church. We find in Galatians 1:6 to 9, "I marvel that ye are so soon removed from Him that called you into the grace of Christ unto another gospel: Which is not another; but there be some that trouble you, and would pervert the gospel of Christ. But though we, or an angel from heaven, preach any other gospel unto you than that which we have preached unto you, let him be accursed. As we said before, so say I now again, If any man preach any other gospel unto you than that ye have received, let him be accursed."

Rev. Rick Nagel pointed out to me that the "Let him be accursed" was repeated twice. This emphasizes the importance of Godly leadership taking their place and calling seriously. We are to defend the faith. Paul said in Philippians 1:17, "I am set for the defense of the gospel." Godly eldership, arise and take your place.

"Judges and officers shalt thou make thee in all thy gates, which the LORD thy God giveth thee, throughout thy tribes: and they shall judge the people with just judgment. Thou shalt not wrest judgment; thou shalt not respect persons, neither take a gift: for a gift doth blind the eyes of the wise, and pervert the words of the righteous" (Deut. 16:18-19).

Almighty God knew the heart of men and the limitations of man, and insisted that judges be placed throughout the tribes of Israel. Today we also require judges placed in our churches. Preaching the word is not the only task of ministers. If that were not true, parts of Matthew 16 and 1 Corinthians 5 would not have been written. It is time to line up with the word of God and make the necessary changes to implement His directives for true revival to come.

"Thus speaketh the LORD of hosts, saying, Execute true judgment, and show mercy and compassion every man to his brother: And oppress not the widow, nor the fatherless, the stranger, nor the poor; and let none of you imagine evil against his brother in your heart. *But they refused to hearken*, and pulled away the shoulder, and stopped their ears, that they should not hear. Yea, they made their hearts as an adamant stone, lest they should hear the law, and the words which the LORD of hosts hath sent in his spirit by the former prophets: *therefore came a great wrath from the LORD of hosts*. Therefore it is come to pass, that as he cried, and they would not hear; so they cried, and I would not hear" (Zech. 7:9-13).

Because we do not set our hearts on true, meaningful judgment, and turn a blind eye and deaf ear, the wrath of God came on them and comes on us. This is a major reason why God does not answer our prayers in times of need. We need to deal with the pain and struggles of people when inequity brings bondage and sorrow.

We need to listen in obedience, and be tough in this matter, as Samuel was before God and Saul. He told Saul, "It repenteth me that I have set up Saul to be king: for he is turned back from following me, and hath not performed my commandments. And Samuel said, Hath the LORD as great delight in burnt offerings and sacrifices, as in obeying the voice of the LORD? Behold, to obey is better than sacrifice, and to hearken than the fat of rams. For rebellion is as the sin of witchcraft, and stubbornness is as iniquity and idolatry. Because thou hast rejected the word of the LORD, he hath also rejected thee from being king. And Agag came unto him delicately. And Agag said, Surely the bitterness of death is past. And Samuel said, As thy sword hath made women childless, so shall thy mother be childless among women. And Samuel hewed Agag in pieces before the LORD in Gilgal" (1 Sam. 15:11 ff).

Today we need to obey the commandment to judge in all matters of the church. Our rebellion and stubbornness in refusing to do so is as the sin of witchcraft. Agag may come to us delicately, but we must have the intestinal fortitude to hew him in pieces. May we worship our God in spirit and Truth. We must judge those within.

Unrighteous eldership and lack of government seem to exist everywhere. People in adultery move to a different home church a few blocks away, and the leadership does nothing. An elder removed due to financial failure, after looking after the church for little money, is not restored, and so on. Lord, help us.
"The robbery of the wicked shall destroy them; because they refuse to do judgment" (Prov. 21:7).

"Wash you, make you clean; put away the evil of your doings from before mine eyes; cease to do evil; Learn to do well; seek judgment, relieve the oppressed, judge the fatherless, plead for the widow (Isai. 1:16).

We must judge within the church by the multitude of counsel and a multiple eldership!

Foundation Principles and Laws of Church Judgment

Principle Number One: Preservation
In 1 Corinthians 5:5, Paul taught the church elders to "deliver such an one unto Satan for the destruction of the flesh, *that the spirit may be saved in the day of the Lord Jesus."* Here we find the measuring stick of judgment.

The purpose of the judgment was the preservation of the spirit of the man. The goal was that his spirit would be saved in the day of the Lord, since it would be lost if he did not change and repent. The correct spirit within the eldership in this judgment was demonstrated by the desire to see this person saved in the end. They judged because they were "taking heed over the flock." They were concerned for the man's soul. They did not judge because of some unrighteous indignation at the sin and sinner involved, or unrighteous anger, but because their caring hearts were filled with sorrow. "For the wrath of man worketh not the righteousness of God." Judgment is not to be carried out with someone standing on their toes screaming "You horrible sinner," but rather out of the spirit of one who mourns. "And ye are puffed up, and have not rather mourned, that he that hath done this deed might be taken away from among you" (1 Cor. 5:2).

We find the same point made to Timothy, where Paul speaks of his dealing with two men and the spirit of that dealing. "Holding faith, and a good conscience; which some having put away concerning faith have made shipwreck: Of whom is Hymenaeus and Alexander; whom I have delivered unto Satan, that they *may learn* not to blaspheme" (1 Tim. 1:19-20).

Some had messed up their good conscience, or spirit man, and Paul bound them over to Satan, for the destruction of the flesh to the intent that they might learn. He did not do this to torture or destroy them, or vent some unholy self-righteous anger or wrath of man. He did it so their spirits might be saved in the day of the Lord.

This is brought out again In 1 Corinthians 5: 6. "Your glorying is not good. Know ye not that a little leaven leaveneth the whole lump?" In other words, do this for the preservation of the church. Allow this immoral stuff to exist without being addressed and the entire church will be infected. Out of love for the church, deal with this. Some would no doubt say, "If I got that personal and direct half of my church might leave, and much of my finances might go with them." Wrong spirit! Dare to discipline. No man can serve two masters. Some will not carry out judgment because they have a weak faith and understanding of the judgment day to come. Others refuse because they have an erroneous doctrine about eternal security, or "once saved always saved."

There are steps of judgment. Peter applied the last step to Ananias and Saphira in Acts 5:4 and 5. "[Ananias] why hast thou conceived this thing in thine heart? thou hast not lied unto men, but unto God. And Ananias hearing these words fell down, and gave up the ghost." Here we see a tremendous and severe judgment under God. The same thing happened with Saphira. I believe Peter did this in obedience, with sorrow. But look at the results:

"And great fear came upon all the church, and upon as many as heard these things. And by the hands of the apostles were many signs and wonders wrought among the people; and they were all with one accord in Solomon's porch. And of the rest durst no man join himself to them: but the people magnified them. And believers were the more added to the Lord, multitudes both of men and women. Inasmuch that they brought forth the sick into the streets, and laid them on beds and couches, that at the least the shadow of Peter passing by might overshadow some of them. There came also a multitude out of the cities" (Acts 15:11-16).

Fear of God resulted. Masses of people were added to the church. None of a wrong spirit dared join themselves. A tremendous anointing came with the faithfulness to judge, and the news of the presence of God brought people in from far and wide.

After considering all of the counsel of God, Peter took this step in judgment. These two had entered into a covenant of deception against God and the Holy Ghost himself. The principle of preservation also applied to the church, and the affect was to quarantine the situation.

The *first* step in judgment is judgment of personal sin, written about in 1 Corinthians 11:30. Here we are told that if we would judge ourselves, God will not have to judge. The secret sin God is dealing with might not even be known outside of you and God. If we would judge ourselves of our own sins, God will not have to judge us. This is said in a different way in Galatians 6:8. "For he that soweth to his flesh shall of the flesh reap corruption; but he that soweth to the Spirit shall of the Spirit reap life everlasting." We also read in Psalm 9:16. "The LORD is known by the judgment which he executeth: the wicked is snared in the work of his own hands."

The *second* step in judgment process, is described in Galatians, where Paul teaches in chapter 6:1, "Brethren, if a man be overtaken in a fault, ye which are spiritual, restore such an one in the spirit of meekness; considering thyself, lest thou also be tempted."

We find a number of steps within this step. First this addressed to "spiritual" men. Others will not apply nor understand this teaching properly. Second, confront the person involved. This takes maturity, the grown up who have learned to speak the truth in love (Eph. 4:15). Next. as we approach the "overtaken one," the goal is *restoration*. Restoration to full fellowship with God and ourselves. He or she is a brother or sister, and needs our help. If and when they are restored, we will love them and receive them and uphold them in honor, remembering only the grace of God and his sea of forgetfulness. We will not remember they failed and forever make them second grade Christians. Total forgiveness and restoration is the goal. This was addressed to "spiritual brethren."

This is where that old Pharisee spirit can rise up. This is just another name for self righteousness, or spiritual pride. The Pharisee spirit says, Let us restore him but never forget he belongs at half status. We will forgive, but never forget. The Pharisee spirit says, "I could never have done what they did. They may have been elders before, but they will never qualify again."

The tough part is approaching such a one with a spirit of true meekness, that says "Yes Lord, I too could be tempted and fail in that very sin. In fact I will approach them with a defensive attitude about my own person, knowing that within my flesh are the germ seeds of sin, and I am capable of being tempted.
The word says to go to the brother. Love protects him. It does not say tell every one else or take it to the church. Mercy! The secrets of the Lord belong unto the Lord. "A talebearer revealeth secrets: but he that is of a faithful spirit concealeth the matter" (Prov. 11: 13).

All these steps need to be cradled in the heart understanding. "He that covereth a transgression seeketh love; but he that repeateth a matter separateth very friends" (Prov. 17:9). Consider this before you make anything public and destroy someone over repented sin and failure. Avoid public exposure; instead, help pick up the broken and wounded person who truly is penitent, and beaten up already by their failure.

I remember the account of a ministry who in integrity confessed to a fellow ministry a past failure in his life. He was applying the instruction that we are to confess our faults one to another and pray one for another. He shared this failure out of a torn and burdened heart. This brother believed in the teaching that we are each other's keepers. In humility, he thought sharing his past failure would be a strengthening of a wall of safety to stand against failure. The ministry who received this confession responded by telling others, and insisted that this be broadcast publicly. I doubt the penitent brother will ever get over this betrayal. God had never exposed the failure, yet a ministry brother did. Forgive him, Lord.

Remember the words of the apostle James. "Brethren, if any of you do err from the truth, and one convert him; Let him know, that he which converteth the sinner from the error of his way shall save a soul from death, and shall hide a multitude of sins (Jms 5:19-20).

The next step is 1 Timothy 5:20 to 21, "Them that sin rebuke before all, that others also may fear. I charge thee before God, and the Lord Jesus Christ, and the elect angels, that thou observe these things without preferring one before another, doing nothing by partiality." These folks must have had a Galatians 6:1 talking to already, and not responded.

Binding a person over to Satan to deal with specific sin would come after all the above steps have been tried. A dealing of instant judgment is applied in different ways depending on circumstances, and one needs to be Holy Ghost led in any of these. Paul spoke blindness over an unbeliever on one occasion (Acts 13:11). I have spoken a sentence of judgment that brought death to a person who was warned twice not to interfere with my ministry of the things of God. He died within a day. On another occasion I found myself speaking judgment over a young man who was warned twice about abusing a man of God. He died within a month. Another time I spoke to a backslidden prophet, not fully knowing the matter, except that he needed to correct something. I told him that if he did not, God would deal with him. I heard from others how he fell sick and never left his sick bed until he passed on. Peter spoke a judgment of death over ones that contrived and covenanted to lie to the Church and the Holy Ghost, and the whole thing was exposed by a word of knowledge.

Some things are to be addressed in a different way. This

includes ways of life like slothfulness and unwillingness to hear sound wisdom. "Now we command you, brethren, in the name of our Lord Jesus Christ, that ye withdraw yourselves from every brother that walketh disorderly, and not after the tradition which he received of us. For yourselves know how ye ought to follow us: for we behaved not ourselves disorderly among you; Neither did we eat any man's bread for naught; but wrought with labor and travail night and day, that we might not be chargeable to any of you....And if any man obey not our word by this epistle, note that man, and have no company with him, that he may be ashamed. Yet count him not as an enemy, but admonish him as a brother" (2 Thes. 3:6-8, 14-15).

We find the same thing written in 1 Timothy 6:3 to 5. We are told to withdraw from some. Again, this is to preserve our person. If the other person is affected positively by our actions, it will bless the other person by preserving them. In any case, this withdrawal would only follow communication about the matter.

The Second Principle of Judgment is Restoration

Judgment of a brother should usually include restoration. I have often seen crushed leadership and people who received judgment by other church leadership, and there was no program for full restoration. That is ungodly judgment. We see the correct attitude of judgment taught by Paul to the Corinthians, where he tells them to deal in love to the very man that he previously told them to bind over to Satan and withdraw themselves from. (2 Cor. 2:6). Sufficient to such a man is this punishment inflicted of many. "So that contrariwise ye ought rather to forgive him, and comfort him, lest perhaps such a one should be swallowed up with overmuch sorrow. Wherefore I beseech you that ye would confirm your love toward him" (2 Cor. 2:7-8).

This admonition to restore a brother should guide our actions, especially when we also consider Galatians 6:1.

We are to keep an eye on those over whom we enact judgment. If there is repentance, draw them in. Confirm your love toward them. We need to let them know that we always loved them, even in judgment. When we restore such a one, we remove every trace of the past and failure. We do not remember him as the one who

160

had an affair with his step-mother, but as a brother to be loved. God took David, who committed adultery and murder to cover the adultery, beyond that day as a prophet before God. A prophet before and after the failure in his life. Restoration? *Total and complete,* and made possible by the blood of Christ! A restored David 'reigned over all Israel; and David executed judgment and justice unto all his people. (2 Sam. 8:15; also 1 Chron. 18:14).

Judgment and justice by a past adulterer and murderer, a prophet of God, and that over a nation? Yes, by the grace of God, he was completely restored.

We need to see God's glory as we stand on the rock by Him, and he presses us into the cleft of that rock (Exod. 33:21). Listen to The Lord speaking forth his name and glory, "the Lord, merciful, gracious long suffering, showing compassion, forgiving iniquity." "Thou therefore, my son, be strong in the grace that is in Christ Jesus" (2 Tim. 2:1). Holy grace, not greasy grace (1 Pet. 1:16).

Rules for Judgment

• Exodus 23:6, "Thou shalt not wrest the judgment of thy poor in his cause." Never be swayed by the financial status of those involved.

• Exodus 23:7, "Keep thee far from a false matter; and the innocent and righteous slay thou not: for I will not justify the wicked." Judge truthfully before God, in righteousness, or be judged yourself as a wicked person.

• Exodus 23:8, "And thou shalt take no gift: for the gift blindeth the wise, and perverteth the words of the righteous." Beware of bribery. This would not have been written if this was not a major area of failure.

• Leviticus 19:15, "Ye shall do no unrighteousness in judgment: thou shalt not respect the person of the poor, nor honor the person of the mighty: but in righteousness shalt thou judge thy neighbor."

• Deuteronomy 1:17, "Ye shall not respect persons in judgment; but ye shall hear the small as well as the great; ye shall not be afraid of the face of man; for the judgment is of God." No special treatment of any kind, only truthful and righteous judgment before God first, then man.

• Zechariah 8:16, "These are the things that ye shall do; Speak ye every man the truth to his neighbor; execute the judgment of truth and peace in your gates."

True judgment brings peace within our gates.

• Isaiah 58:6-7, "Is not this the fast that I have chosen? *to loose the bands of wickedness, to undo the heavy burdens, and to let the oppressed go free, and that ye break every yoke?* Is it not to deal thy bread to the hungry, and that thou bring the poor that are cast out to thy house? when thou seest the naked, that thou cover him."

The true worship of God entails dealing with people where the rubber meets the pavement on life's gritty streets. This involves dealing with oppression of the defenseless, guiding the weak, and being a champion for the weary on behalf of God. True worship entails breaking yokes in addition to feeding the hungry, poor and naked.

Apostolic Judgment

"Why hast thou conceived this thing in thine heart? thou hast not lied unto men, but unto God. And Ananias hearing these words fell down, and gave up the ghost: and great fear came on all them that heard these things" (Acts 5:5-6). God has not changed. This judgment brought a blessing to the church in many ways.

"For I verily, as absent in body, but present in spirit, have judged already, as though I were present, concerning him that hath so done this deed" (1 Cor. 5:3). The apostle may not be present, but his authority is spiritual before God.

"But when Peter was come to Antioch, I withstood him to the face, because he was to be blamed. For before that certain came from James, he did eat with the Gentiles: but when they were come, he withdrew and separated himself, fearing them which were of the circumcision. And the other Jews dissembled likewise with him; inasmuch that Barnabas also was carried away with their dissimulation. But when I saw that they walked not uprightly according to the truth of the gospel, I said unto Peter before them all" (Galatians 2:11-14). Apostles will correct one another, publicly if the sin was publicly perpetrated, affecting others.

Blessings of Judgment

"*Blessed are they that keep judgment,* and he that doeth righteousness at all times. Remember me, O LORD, with the favor that thou bearest unto thy people" (Ps. 106:3-4). We may expect the blessing of God and favor if we are obedient to enact judgment.

"Thus saith the LORD, Keep ye judgment, and do justice: for my salvation is near to come, and my righteousness to be revealed. Blessed is the man that doeth this, and the son of man that layeth hold on it (Isai 56:1-2). By keeping judgment in the church, we can expect to see God's salvation and blessing upon us.

"The way of peace they know not; and there is no judgment in their goings: they have made them crooked paths: whosoever goeth therein shall not know peace. Therefore is judgment far from us, neither doth justice overtake us: we wait for light, but behold obscurity" (Isai. 59:8). Peace will be our portion and obscurity will evaporate. Hallelujah!!!

"I will also command the clouds that they rain no rain upon it. For the vineyard of the LORD of hosts is the house of Israel, and the men of Judah his pleasant plant: and he looked for judgment, but behold oppression; for righteousness, but behold a cry (Isai. 56:7-8). When God sees true judgment taking place in God's vineyard and pleasant plant, the Israel of God, the church, the latter rain and anointing will fall. May we repent and believe and act on God's word.

Finally, Isaiah 61:8 and 9, "For I the LORD love judgment. I hate robbery for burnt offering; and I will direct their work in truth, and I will make an everlasting covenant with them. And their seed shall be known among the Gentiles, and their offspring among the people: all that see them shall acknowledge them, that they are the seed which the Lord has blessed." These blessed are those who love our God and judgment.

Chapter 13

CHURCH JUDGMENT EXAMPLE: DIVORCE

Much has been written on the topic of divorce, including many books about divorce recovery. I am an advocate for recovery and God's restoration. This includes forgiveness of sins and failure. In divorce, some do not have failure, or are not to be held responsible, having done their Godly all. Due to lack of church judgment, the innocent are declared guilty, while the church is guilty of not declaring the innocent.

Basically, God is against divorce and the Word of God calls marriage a covenant (Mal. 2:14). Having said that, I must add that God accepts divorce as an undesirable solution where no other solution is available. *God Himself will enter into divorce over wrong.* If we do not see this as sound scriptural theology, we will not be capable of calling any divorce righteous or upholding the innocent. We should know the whole counsel of the Word of God on this subject.

One of the major traumas resulting from divorce is guilt. This guilt within the divorced is applied towards God, as well as man. If we correctly understand theology on this subject, we will be enabled to minister to the divorced. How can we minister to those involved, when we cover all with a gray blanket, and no white and black are established? To seek out understanding of the scriptural values on this topic is Godly and essential. This means that we need to search out theology to enable us to minister in the rights and wrongs in regards to this awful dilemma of human failure. Many wounded brothers and sisters surround us, walking in continuous pain. Much of this is due to the apathy and guilt of wimp church leadership, and multiplied due to a wrong and immature church leadership structure.

To sum this up, lacking theological understanding, lacking heart for the hurt in the flock, gutless leadership who will not judge and call a spade a spade, and a wrong leadership structure combine to make a great lack in the church, when dealing with the divorced.

Jeremiah 5:4, "Therefore I said, Surely these are poor; they are foolish: for they know not the way of the LORD, nor the judgment of their God. I will get me unto the great men, and will speak unto them; for they have known the way of the LORD, and the 'judgment of their God': but these have altogether broken the yoke, and burst the bonds. Wherefore a lion out of the forest shall slay them."

When we lack great men and no judgment goes forth, the people perish by lions.

Divorce takes place in the church as well as the world, and we need Godly guidelines to deal with the people caught in this thorny, painful ground. There are countless tears shed over any divorce, both in anger and sorrow. My efforts here are limited to some theological observations, eldership responsibilities, and church judgment.

Somehow dealing with this topic is like walking through a mine field. You never know when you are going to step on the wrong spot in someone's thinking and get a severe explosion. Due to the extreme pain and mangling of human lives, and out of love for all the church, I want to eliminate some of this disaster area. At the very least, I want to mitigate some of the damage to both the divorced and separated, and bystanders.

A large part of the problem is the lack of righteous judgment in the church. Much of this is no doubt due to a lack of knowledge and wrong theology. In the Old Testament, the priesthood did not just minister to the Lord. They discerned among the people, and determined what was clean and unclean. They also judged matters, and were accessible in the place of judgment in all matters of controversy. This meant determining right and wrong between members of the family of God. This principle is still in force, and we, the called Royal Priesthood need to stand in the same place within the congregation today.

Ezekiel 44:23 and 24, "And they shall teach my people the difference between the holy and profane, and cause them to discern between the unlcean and the clean. And in controversy they shall stand in judgment; and they shall judge it according to my judgments: and they shall keep my laws and my statutes in all mine assemblies; and they shall hallow my sabbaths."

Let's establish an essential truth. Does God actually divorce himself from people?

Yes! Jeremiah 3:7 and 8, "And I said after she had done all these things, Turn thou unto me. But she returned not. And her treacherous sister Judah saw it. And I saw, when for all the causes whereby backsliding Israel committed adultery I had put her away, and given her a bill of divorce; yet her treacherous sister Judah feared not, but went and played the harlot also."

God is Holy and Righteous, and is named by these names. God also is a God of covenant, and when you get saved, He enters into a covenant with you. There are conditions to the covenant God makes. God made covenant with Israel and gave the promise of blessings and life, as well as curses and death (Deut. 28:2 & 15). Note that the promised curses are as real in verse 15 as the blessings of verse two. Note that the curses lead to death if there is no repentance. We see the results of God divorcing Israel over the last two thousand years, culminating with the Holocaust.

This divorce was referred to by Paul, when he stated in Romans 11:25 that blindness or hardening of the heart has come to Israel until the times of the Gentiles shall be fulfilled. Some Jews will be saved when they repent, but it seems to be few.

God will judge the one that breaks His covenant, and ultimately, when there is no righteous response, divorce himself from such a one. We read about the divorce and results in First Corinthians 10:1 to 12.

"Moreover, brethren, I would not that ye should be ignorant, how that all our fathers were under the cloud, and all passed through the sea; And were all baptized unto Moses in the cloud and in the sea; And did all eat the same spiritual meat; And did all drink the same spiritual drink: for they drank of that spiritual Rock that followed them: and that Rock was Christ. But with many of them God was not well pleased: for they were overthrown in the wilderness. Now these things were our examples, to the intent we should not lust after evil things, as they also lusted. Neither be ye idolaters, as were some of them; as it is written, The people sat down to eat and drink, and rose up to play. Neither let us commit fornication, as some of them committed, and fell in one day three and twenty thousand. Neither let us tempt Christ, as some of them also tempted, and were destroyed of serpents. Neither murmur ye, as some of them also murmured, and were destroyed of the destroyer. Now all these things happened unto them for ensamples: and they are written for our admonition, upon whom the ends of the world are come. Wherefore let him that thinketh he standeth take heed lest he fall."

Notice that verses three to six state that God was displeased with many of these children of Abraham, covenant people, circumcised and all, and overthrew them in the wilderness. These overthrown are our examples. These people were baptized into Moses and the cloud. The cloud (that covered them in the day time), and which followed them, was Christ.

This judgment came on them because of what they did. This applies to us as well.

Isaiah 49:26 and 50:1, "I the LORD am thy Savior and thy Redeemer, the mighty One of Jacob. Thus saith the LORD, *Where is the bill of your mother's divorcement, whom I have put away?* or which of my creditors is it to whom I have sold you? Behold, for your iniquities have ye sold yourselves, and for your transgressions is your mother put away."

The Lord and redeemer of Jacob put Israel away because of their doings. The church needs to put some people away because of their doings. We who preach that we receive power when the Holy Ghost comes upon us are given this responsibility. Those who labor and major in eschatology need to consider that the redeemer of Jacob spoke in Jeremiah 16:15 and 16. He foretold the hunter who would bring Israel to their native land fulfilling the words of Christ (Lk. 21:24). Hitler was that hunter and put millions of the children of Israel to a terrible death. Eschatology is important, but something else is more important. We need to see the judgment of God in our church by a multiple eldership!

We need to perform the judgment of God among His people, and if we would, God would not have to judge. We need to judge ourselves and others with the principles of preservation, love, and restoration in mind. When we do not judge ourselves, God will have to, and for this reason some of you are sickly and die.

168

The same principle applies to the church and the leadership. When leaders refuse to judge and set at right issues of wrong, people die (1 Cor. 11:30, Jer. 5:5). May we love our people enough to learn the principles and theology of Godly judgment in the church, including marital problems and divorce.

Malachi 2: 10 to 13, "Have we not all one father? hath not one God created us? why do we deal treacherously every man against his brother, by profaning the covenant of our fathers? Judah hath dealt treacherously, and an abomination is committed in Israel and in Jerusalem ; for Judah hath profaned the holiness of the LORD which He loved (past tense), and hath married the daughter of a strange god. The LORD will cut off the man that doeth this, the master and the scholar, out of the tabernacles of Jacob, and him that offereth an offering unto the LORD of hosts. And this have ye done again, covering the altar of the LORD with tears."

Judah, out of whom Christ was born, treacherously left off loving the Lord and married the daughter of a strange god. God's promise to them was cut off. This was irrespective of scholar or minister, and their religious tears and offerings did not alter God's heart or judgment. I believe that the God who does not change did this with the knowledge that a little leaven leavens the whole lump (1 Cor. 5:6). We need to judge right and wrong in the church.

Some will quote Malachi 2:15, where we are reminded not to deal treacherously with the wife of our youth. We are also reminded of the contents of verse sixteen, where God speaks of His dislike of "putting away." These scriptures can also be applied towards men being abused by their wives. Sometimes a woman can act out of a root of bitterness by which many are defiled (Heb. 12:15). When this situation exists, subtle things and reactions thwart and resist a husband. Should she not be willing to address these things, the marriage will be in jeopardy. When one of the two partners inwardly digs in their heels and refuses to make themselves available for communication and counseling, the marriage is on slippery ground. It is a sin to hold silence and act in subtleties and untruth, just as it is a sin to put away. We do not have the right to withhold honest, open, caring conversation. Some actions can be the root cause of putting away. In a divorce action, the real divorce usually took place long before the papers were signed. Whoever filed for the divorce and initiated the paper work may simply be the one who mopped up the floor after the spill. The real issues are to be sorted out by those involved, and when they are unable to do so, this must be dealt with by and through the church. If one is unwilling to do so, that one is ungodly, as anyone who will not listen to the church.

God's New Testament Directive

In the church we need to know and understand what is written in 1 Corinthians chapter seven. We find instructions to the married in the church. Verses one to eleven are written to a distinct group. Verses 12 to 15 are written to an entirely different group.

Verses one to eleven are written to the church, Corinth AND US, and apply to two married believers. This is doubly clear when we read the line of distinction in verse twelve, "to the rest speak I." "To the rest" defines a different group and verse twelve and thirteen describes them. The rules are clear for both groups. We need to judge all matters with these scriptural distinctions and rules in mind.

To the two married in Christ, the rules are to try to avoid separation and then not to remarry, but work out their differences, and be reconciled (verses 10-11).

To the rest, a different set of rules apply. A huge difference. Read it. In verse twelve and thirteen we read *if*. IF! If the unbeliever is pleased to dwell with the believer, let the believer not leave the unbeliever. Let us face this head on and not "wimp out." That means if the unbeliever is not pleased to dwell with a believer, that the believer is free to depart, and ultimately, a brother or a sister is not under bondage in such cases: but God hath called us to peace (verse 15).

May we have the intestinal fortitude to declare them not under bondage. May we have the bowels of mercy to judge the matter, and as an authoritative ministry eldership declare them not under bondage (Phil. 2:1). FREE! Free to marry or not marry. The only limits on those who are loosed from such a situation is the same as those that apply to any child of God. Marry "in the Lord" (1 Cor. 7:39).

Some get all hung up on "if the unbeliever depart" (verse 15). Yes, the believer should stay in the marriage if at all possible and attempt to win the unbeliever to Christ. However, they are not to consider the marriage a prison complete with ball and chain. The unbeliever may not want to depart and may want to physically stay. The physical benefit package may have sexual, financial, maid or Mr. Fix-It advantages, not necessarily in this order. God himself defined adultery as something more than a physical sex act outside of a covenant relationship (Math. 5:28). We need to consider a host of other scriptures as well.

Jeremiah 3:8, "I saw for all the causes whereby backsliding Israel committed adultery I had put her away, and given her a bill of divorce."

God said FOR ALL THE CAUSES. This all is more than one. The affects of this scripture and judgment of divorce can be seen even now.

Jeremiah 23:14, "I have seen also in the prophets of Jerusalem an horrible thing: they commit adultery , and walk in lies: they strengthen also the hands of evildoers, that none doth return from his wickedness: they are all of them unto me as Sodom, and the inhabitants thereof as Gomorrah."

Ezekiel 23:36 to 37, "The LORD said moreover unto me; Son of man, wilt thou judge Aholah and Aholibah? yea, declare unto them their abominations; That they have committed adultery, and blood is in their hands, and with their idols have they committed adultery [not physical sex], and have also caused their sons, whom they bare unto me, to pass for them through the fire, to devour them."

A PERSON MAY PHYSICALLY STAY AND SIMULTA-NEOUSLY LEAVE IN MANY OTHER WAYS. You can be somewhere physically, while your heart—your attention, care, and focus—is far away. Let us balance "if the unbeliever depart" with the entire text (1 Cor. 7: 12,13,15). They are free to go if the unbeliever is not genuinely happy to dwell with them. Verses 12 to 15 especially apply to the unbeliever being unhappy with the believer's faith walk, and the results of living that faith walk. These things include devotions, church and prayer meeting attendance, and Christian friends and fellowship. The church leadership is to stand for, encourage, and uphold the believer in their rightful "rights." To uphold the unbeliever in their supposed rights, by limiting the believer from these rights, is blindness and blasphemy. 1 Corinthians 7 was written to direct and uphold the believer in their rights. There are no scriptures written to the unbeliever about marriage or any other matter, in this chapter or the entire Bible! Only the message of salvation is directed to the unbeliever.

Let's uphold the believer in the scriptural admonishment of that *God has called them to peace* (verse 15). How this peace has been destroyed in the lives of some believers is a horror story beyond belief. Some ungodly leaders have told believers, supposedly by God's authority, to put up with some awful things. Some have told believers that if the unbeliever does not want them to go to church, stay home and pray, and ignore thereby the scriptural admonishment that we are not to forsake the assembling together of ourselves (Heb. 10:25). Some have told the believer to comply with ungodly demands of the unbeliever.

May God forgive them! Judge righteous judgment. Others have told believers it is their responsibility to absorb abuse, physically and emotionally, applied by the unbeliever. These so-called Godly leaders are severely misguided in their ungodly opinions and need to repent. They need to go to those whom they have abused with their bad counsel and weep as they beg for forgiveness. Jeremiah had words for these leaders. "I have seen also in the prophets of Jerusalem an horrible thing: they commit adultery, and walk in lies: *they strengthen also the hands of evildoers*" (Jer. 23:14).

Uphold and encourage the believer in their God-ordained right to live for Him and serve Him. *Devil and unbeliever, back off God's property.*

I know a woman who was badly beaten by her alcoholic husband, and spoke with tears to her pastor about the situation. The cream and make-up applied did not hide her black eye or cracked lip. This had happened several times. The pastor told her it was her cross to bear, to go home, pray for her husband, and win him to Christ. I withstood the temptation to walk into his office, punch him in the nose, and tell him it was his duty to put up with this behavior, and pray for me.

She came to me through a mutual acquaintance, and I promptly advised her to move to other premises of safety, and deal with the problem from there. I also pointed out her scriptural rights according to 1 Corinthians chapter seven, including her rights to divorce him if she could not live in peace with him. If she did, she was free to marry a Godly man. Tough ground? Include this chapter in your theology and "hew Agag" (1 Sam. 15:33), if you must.

This in no wise eliminates the believer's Godly responsibility to love the unbeliever and attempt to win him or her to Christ, but know your rights and liberty in Christ. We need to see a clear separation of those in the world and those not of the world (Jn. 17:15,16). We need a mature, multiple, five-fold ministry and eldership to judge and care for the needs of the church flock.

Scriptural Divorce

Some have only heard and read Matthew 19:9, where we read, "And I say to you, whosoever shall put away his wife, except it be for fornication, and shall marry another, commits adultery." Because this is all that is presented to the majority of Christians, those entering into divorce are locked into having to prove physical adultery on the part of their spouse. Let us at least uphold those who are victims of adultery and wind up in divorce. We must declare them innocent. Let us also consider all scriptures on this topic.

There are many more scriptures on this topic, and we need to apply the whole counsel of God to have a righteous and Godly dealing with those involved in the church. We read the following in the Old Testament.

Ruth 4:8 to 11, "Therefore the kinsman said unto Boaz, Buy it for thee. So he drew off his shoe. And Boaz said unto the elders, and unto all the people, Ye are witnesses this day, that I have bought all that was Elimelech's, and all that was Chilion's and Mahlon's, of the hand of Naomi. Moreover Ruth the Moabitess, the wife of Mahlon, have I purchased to be my wife, to raise up the name of the dead upon his inheritance, that the name of the dead be not cut off from among his brethren, and from the gate of his place: ye are witnesses this day. *And all the people that were in the gate, and the elders,* said, We are witnesses."

Deuteronomy 25:7 to 9, "And if the man like not to take his brother's wife, then let his brother's wife go up to the gate unto the elders, and say, My husband's brother refuseth to raise up unto his brother a name in Israel, he will not perform the duty of my husband's brother. Then *the elders of his city shall call him,* and speak unto him: and if he stand to it, and say, I like not to take her; Then shall his brother's wife come unto him in the presence of the elders, and loose his shoe from off his foot, and spit in his face, and shall answer and say, So shall it be done unto that man that will not build up his brother's house."

We read here that matters involving the rights and wrongs of these situations were settled by taking off of the shoe, and in one case by spitting in the face of the guilty person. This was finalized before the elders. Matters of right and wrong were judged and witnessed by and before elders then and should be now. We need to see some shoes being removed in the sight of the elders. Some will immediately say, "that's Old Testament." Deuteronomy 25:7 was God's directive on how to deal with this matter. People still have the same problems. The difference is that the past priesthood and elders are replaced with the Jesus' ministry, today's five-fold eldership.

How does this apply to the New Testament church? We clearly read in Matthew our Lord's commandment about dealing with people's sins and problems involving each other.

Matthew 18:15 to 18, "Moreover if thy brother shall trespass against thee, go and tell him his fault between thee and him alone: if he shall hear thee, thou hast gained thy brother. But if he will not hear thee, then take with thee one or two more, that in the mouth of two or three witnesses every word may be established. And if he shall neglect to hear them, tell it unto the church: *but if he neglect to hear the church, let him be unto thee as an heathen man and a publican.* Verily I say unto you, Whatsoever ye shall bind on earth shall be bound in heaven."

The church has in some cases provided marriage counseling. This is a help to some, and the intent is Godly. However, this does not reflect the authority of the church. We bind on earth and in heaven. To help sort out problems, listening with care, and counseling prayerfully is charitable, Godly, brotherly love in action. This also shows humility and a spirit of submission on the part of those seeking counseling. In the case of wrong doing, the church must insist on repentance, and defend the innocent. The church eldership is to judge matters of wrongdoing, and see that these areas are corrected. If the unrepentant person will not listen, and continues in his or her sin and error, the elders must declare the innocence of the party that is not guilty, and treat the unyielding and unrepentant person as unrighteous.

There are several things in Matthew 18 we need to consider. *First*, we need to understand that this is just as valid if it read "if your sister trespass against thee." The laws of righteousness and holiness apply to men and women alike. Salvation is an individual matter. A woman may be saved while her husband is not (1 Cor. 7:13).

Second, we need to understand that if your brother or sister sins against you also applies to husbands and wives. The wife as well as the husband is to find a shelter of righteous protection and a defense of right and wrong in the church.

Third, this is upheld in the Old Testament as well as the New. Observe the foregoing quoted in Deuteronomy 25:7, *"let his brother's wife go up to the gate unto the elders, and say..."* She approached the elders to receive righteous judgment in a matter regarding marriage. The church is to be approachable by those who are being wronged and abused in a "Christian" marriage. If we are not, we are co-responsible for the demise of the marriage and any eventual divorce because we did not defend the innocent and set a standard of righteousness. Out of love for God and man, may we see our responsibilities in this area and take heed of the flock.

Fourth, in this holy process, you may conclude one of the partners of the marriage is an innocent victim, willing to address any potential area of wrong. Meanwhile the spouse is unwilling to be counseled or face issues in the marriage, and avoids conversation by stymieing meetings, or refusing to address issues of importance to their spouse. This partner may even refuse to allow the church to address them and discuss issues. This is acting totally outside the laws of love. Love wants to understand and work out difficulties to bring peace and unity. Are we aware of the church's God-given, holy authority?

Fifth, when one of the partners refuses to listen to the Godly counsel of the Church, *we may have to treat that one as a heathen, or as an unsaved person.* Consider that. Our judgment had better be righteous. The people submitting to the church for judgment had better be transparent and Godly. If the church binds a judgment on earth, it will be bound in heaven.

We need to have Godly and mature ministries and elders who are responsible under God. Taking heed of the flock is serious business. The flock might take God and holiness more seriously when the ministry and leadership do.

Sixth, should a past brother or sister not listen to the church, be judged, and treated as a publican and heathen, the same rules of truth written in 1 Corinthians 7:12 to 15 apply to that person. In other words, the one treated as a heathen and publican unbeliever (Math. 18:17) will now also be in the unbeliever category of I Corinthians chapter seven. Treating the person who will not listen to the church as an unbeliever is according to the command of Christ. Taking someone to the church was a directive and command, not an option. Read it. We tend to ignore this, treat this scripture as an option, and sin by doing so.

The break up of that marriage, under these conditions, leaves the believer free of condemnation and free to remarry. Do we see the necessity to judge right and wrong in marriage? The church eldership is set in place to protect the innocent and determine right from wrong (1 Cor. 6:5). We are to deal in justice, and uphold the cause of the innocent before God.

Examples of Wrong Judgment

Earlier I mentioned a wonderful church secretary whom I know, who is not serving God the way she used to, and frankly is "backslidden." I do not justify her, yet I understand how she got there. Some should shake in their boots with fear, if they face the fact that they have offended one of the little ones and caused one of these little ones to stumble (Math. 18:6). She was serving God and woke up one morning to find hubby gone with some sweet young thing. I do not know all the details, but the church leadership never publicly declared him guilty or innocent. They only removed her from her faithful place of service to God because of "what the people and the world might think." Imagine a divorced person being a church secretary. Imagine also the holy anger of the Lord over this travesty of justice. Crucified by husband and abandoned by the church, and all of that supposedly over Godly appearances which were in fact ungodly . I did not hear of a plan for restitution. I also did not hear of judgment or any sort of public announcement over this situation. In the Deuteronomy and Ruth examples all the people knew and approved the verdict. All this happened in a "full Gospel church," which loses credibility to be called that. No righteous judgment.

This morning, while writing this very chapter on my word processor, I received a long distance call from a young Christian lady struggling with what to advise her friend, who lives near my town and is facing a probable divorce. (Coincidence or direction?)

The friend is a young woman of a "Christian couple." She got saved in her teens, and her husband was raised in a genuine Christian home. My caller explained this story, which may or may not be entirely objective, and would need to be searched out in depth by the ministry involved to determine the facts.

Apparently, the shaky marriage had a number of problems. The "Christian" husband tells his wife that if she does not provide the sex he requires when he wants it, he will go elsewhere to get his needs met, and she will be at fault. Her husband had recently admitted to child molestation of his younger sister. Among other things, he threatened that if she got out of the marriage, she would have to leave the kids. He added, "If you leave with them, I will call the police and tell them you have abducted them. If you leave them with me I will tell the proper government office that you abandoned them."

My immediate response was to tell the caller to advise the young Christian women to go to her authorities, first of all to the Godly father-in-law, then the church. Apparently the Godly father-in-law was biased by his son's negative stories and she had no confidence in approaching him. As for the church, she had already tried that. The church had sent a genuine man of God whom I respect, a minister within their church, to counsel the two of them. According to the wife, the counseling went fine until the husband was confronted in areas that he did not want to discuss, and refused to go to any more sessions. After that the young woman went to a Christian lady counselor who seemed to be doing her level best in applying wisdom.

If they get divorced, there will be immediate tearing of many hearts, and the believers in that church will cast their gray blankets, and those involved will justify one or the other. Polarization of friends and family will result, including polarization within the family of God. Confusion will reign. Gossip will fly. Every church with no Godly judgment is widespread with gossip.

The real answer should lie in the church. The ministry whom I respect should never have dropped the ball. He knew of the pain and heartaches of the young couple involved. In taking heed over the flock, he should have stayed with this situation until it was resolved. If he felt inadequate, he should have involved other elders. He should never allow the young man to choose whether he would come for counseling, as long as the elder was not satisfied with the conclusion.

Perhaps he could have the Christian father and mother-in-law sit in on an open conversation to dispel infighting and expose truth. In any case, he should insist on the young husband's responsibility to attend church "judgment counseling," adding authority and not just advice. A Godly dealing at this level, facing the ISSUES involved and not just dispensing forgiveness, in a right and gentle but firm attitude, would bring an eventual Godly end to the matter. We pray and hope for a positive conclusion. However, if one of the parties will not listen to the church, they must be rebuked publicly, and in some cases bound over to Satan. Only then have we done all we can to correct the wrong.

That is our duty in the nitty gritty of church life. Always attempt restoration with true peace. If this can not be achieved, those who refuse to face counseling and heed the church must be treated as publicans and HEATHENS. If they simply move to another church, do not worry about it. Send the judgment of God with them, and trust God. If we act, God will act. We are not condemning them to hell. That's God's arena of judgment, and He knows the end of the matter. We desire to see them repent and turn. Any church they flee to will face problems if they allow them peaceful refuge, because they don't want to upset anyone and are looking for cash flow and numbers. God will ultimately deal with them and us according to our works. A proper, functioning eldership will seek out the background of the new arrivals, and deal with them.

CLEAR THE INNOCENT! IDENTIFY THE GUILTY! FORGIVE THE PENITENT! We need a multiple, Godly, mature eldership and five-fold ministry to fulfill this responsibility.

Isaiah 50:1, "Thus saith the LORD, Where is the bill of your mother's divorcement, whom I have put away? or which of my creditors is it to whom I have sold you? Behold, for your iniquities have ye sold yourselves, and for your transgressions is your mother put away."

This is self explanatory, telling us that *God reacted to the actions of the person involved.* Let us see this in the following scriptures, and our response and acceptable reactions to other's actions.

1 Corinthians 7:12 to 15, "But to the rest speak I, not the Lord: If any brother hath a wife that believeth not, and she be pleased to dwell with him, let him not put her away. And the woman which hath an husband that believeth not, and if he be pleased to dwell with her, let her not leave him. For the unbelieving husband is sanctified by the wife, and the unbelieving wife is sanctified by the husband: else were your children unclean; but now are they holy. But if the unbelieving depart, let him depart. *A brother or a sister is not under bondage in such cases:* but God hath called us to peace."

The word *bondage* in this chapter is the same word taken from the Greek word that was translated *bondage* in Galatians 4:3, speaking of the law. There we are taught our freedom from the law. This means we are severed from and totally free of it. May we act and judge accordingly we deal with those involved.

Some people press the point that the believer should stay no matter what may transpire within the marriage. Yes, the believer will be a sanctifying, or holy and cleansing force within the marriage (verse 14). However, salvation is an individual matter, and this chapter does not speak of automatic salvation for the unbeliever. This simply means the believer has a cleansing influence on the unbeliever. Whether one stays in the marriage, and they should if it is at all possible, is still predicated on the condition of whether the unbeliever is pleased to dwell with the believer. Furthermore, since God has called us to peace (verse 15), and he specifically draws our attention to this in the context of an unequally yoked marriage relationship, may we consider all of the above in this light. Should the unbeliever's displeasure of the believer's life and walk make the believer unable to live in peace, if the marriage dissolves to allow the believer to live in peace, the believer is not in bondage.

Matthew 5:28, "But I say unto you, That whosoever looketh on a woman to lust after her hath committed adultery with her already in his heart."

Mental and emotional abuse, and unfaithfulness can be expressed by the eyes. Some may not believe in divorce and are limited to their relationship within the marriage due to this, but their eyes are outside the marriage. This is adultery before God. May we strive for Job's covenant. Job made a covenant with his eyes not to look upon a maid (Job 31:1). Since all have sinned and come short of the glory of God, we are all tempted to think, if not act, in a wrong manner. We are encouraged to have a renewed mind (Rom. 12:2). It is a battle to overcome the flesh, no matter how spiritual we may think we are. Praise God He forgives and cleanses us with the blood.

Matthew 19:29, "And every one that hath forsaken houses, or brethren, or sisters, or father, or mother, or wife [who obviously did not want to seek God and ministry the same as their spouse], or children, or lands, for my name's sake, shall receive an hundredfold, and shall inherit everlasting life."

This could not be applied to any situation other than a marriage partner who did not flow with serving God, otherwise there would be a transgression of 1 Timothy 5:8. This marriage partner blocked and undermined the ministry of a Godly, determined person, who paid the price. In some cases, this price is huge.

There will be failure, lack of sensitivity, impatience and wrong, on the part of all people involved in marriage. The wrong should be dealt with and forgiven. In dealing with wrong, nobody has the right to not listen or hear in full the struggle within their spouse. No spouse has the right to deny the request of their marriage partner to attend Godly counseling to help communicate and deal with problems. No one has the right to resist coming before the church on the request of their husband or wife, regardless of their opinion of right and wrong within the marriage. No church has the right to refuse anyone a thorough hearing, or refuse to deal with issues of right and wrong. We are human and imperfect, but these ground rules are basic, Godly, and correct for all.

May we apply true, Godly, sensitive and gracious judgment in the church of Jesus Christ. May we love God and the family of God enough. May we attempt to keep a matter confidential and help. Love covers a multitude of sins. Yet may we be strong to deal with issues at any level of grace, including severity, and to turn the impenitent, with total restoration in mind. Praise God!

Chapter 14

KINGDOM FINANCES

We are the blessed people of the world. For those who look with faith towards God, and live righteously before our God, there is an ongoing blessing of His care for us. Jesus taught how the tiny sparrow is cared for and how much more we are cared for. Countless Christians can tell stories of our God's mighty intervention in their lives and how He has met their needs. Our faith is tested in finances as well as other areas of our lives.

This testing of our faith involves learning to give financially to God and the family of God. We are even taught to use the "mammon" of this world to win people for eternity (Lk. 16:7). The New Testament clearly teaches the blessings associated with giving faithfully (2 Cor. 9:6), and few ministries would deny this truth. That is the only agreement I can reach with them on this topic.

The church teachings in general are out of balance in regard to teachings on financial giving, and especially the distribution of Kingdom moneys.

There are well over one hundred (100) texts in the New Testament on the subject of finances, and only half a dozen are sermon topics in ninety-nine percent of churches. The imbalance is profound, and as we take the lid off of this smelly can, let us consider why the vast majority of scripture on this topic is not preached. Discern the motive in the following few pages.

My heart is burdened for the church and to see what God intended for the church to become a reality. God intended to provide the church with a royal banquet table of the multiple ministries and eldership. This will not function unless we come to terms with this topic. Let's look closer at the "sacred cow."

Minister's Rights to Finances and Scriptural Support

One of the popular half dozen scriptures dealing with finances is Acts 20:35, "Remember the words of the Lord Jesus, how He said, *It is more blessed to give than to receive.*"

Ninety nine percent of the time, this text is quoted to encourage the laity, congregation, or flock to give to the church. One hundred percent of the time it is quoted out of context. You have no doubt heard this text at offering time. My teachers taught me that a text taken out of context is a pretext. This text was not written for this usage, and is used as a pretext for minister support.

This text was addressed to the eldership and ministries, *not* the congregation. However much the principle applies to all, it is never preached with the intent for which it is written. In context the elders and ministry were told to work with their hands, and give to the needy people! Have you heard this scripture used this way? If you look this up and agree my observations are correct, continue reading.

In Acts 20:17, Paul calls for the elders of the church of Ephesus to meet with him. The plurality eldership (ministers) came, and the rest of this chapter is spoken expressly to them. Since all scripture is given by inspiration of God, and is profitable for doctrine, for reproof, for correction, for instruction in righteousness (2 Tim. 3:16), this applies not only to Corinth and Galatia, but to our local church as well. Time does not change the truth. Let's set this doctrine straight and be instructed in righteousness.

Among other things, in Acts 20:29 and 30, Paul warns the eldership about savage wolves, and how elders from among this very eldership ministry would rise up speaking perverse untruths and gain a following. He then teaches Holy Ghost truths I have never heard a sermon on, dealing with financial matters. These scriptures are part of the unpreached ninety-four percent.

Acts 20: 33 to 37, "I have coveted no one's silver or gold or apparel. Yes, you yourselves know that these hands have provided for my necessities, and for those who were with me. I have shown you in every way, BY LABORING LIKE THIS, YOU MUST SUPPORT THE WEAK. AND remember the words of the Lord

Jesus, that He said, It is more blessed to give than to receive. And when he had said these things, he knelt down and prayed with them all. Then they all [the Ephesian elders and ministers] wept freely, and fell on Paul's neck and kissed him."

"These hands" were the hands of Paul who wrote half the New Testament. He told the elders (ministers) to pay attention and follow the example GIVEN TO THEM OVER THE LAST THREE YEARS. He told them work with their hands to supply the needs of the flock, and while they did it, the Lord Jesus wanted them to remember that it is more blessed to give than to receive. Hello!

Elders working. Remember the elders called to meet with Paul were the multiple ministry leadership, the same men given directions in verse 28 to take heed of the flock and teach the flock. They were also reminded that the Holy Ghost had made them overseers. *Now these same elders were instructed to supply the needs of the weak, and give to the flock.* These same elders were to remember the words of the Lord Jesus Christ that it is better for them to give and support the weak, than receive. Yet these very words are consistently used to encourage the flock to give to the elder(s), instead of the scriptural usage.

If this got your attention, and you are still reading on, and you are an elder/minister, you must desire truth and righteousness, and want to see God's Kingdom come on earth.

The next scripture to consider of the often quoted half dozen is 1 Corinthians 9:13 to 15. "Do ye not know that they which minister about holy things live of the things of the temple? and they which wait at the altar are partakers with the altar? Even so hath the Lord ordained that they which preach the gospel should live of the gospel. But I have used none of these things: neither have I written these things, that it should be so done unto me."

The first part of this text is correctly quoted to support a minister's right to be upheld financially by the believers, and we hear this portion quoted constantly. However, I have yet to hear this balanced and in context from any pulpit, or presented with the rest of the statements. The author under the anointing continued with, *"But I have used none of these things: neither have I written these things, that it should be so done unto me."* When have you, especially you ministers and elders, heard this text read and preached for you to consider in your life?

Paul, who said of himself that he labored (in the gospel) more abundantly than all of the other apostles, said that he did not use this right. This tremendous man of God ministered in and lived with this church for three years, determined not to take any money from them during his stay. That is the rest of this often quoted text. Perhaps we should study why he said this, and how and when he applied this, and when he did accept money. I have not heard this topic addressed in a meaningful way. We will pursue this in the next few pages.

Offerings taken on Sundays are to support the pastor and church overhead. Right? We know this is true about our Sunday giving, right? *Wrong!* There is not one New Testament text to support this. There are few texts in the New Testament about Sunday offerings, and we use these in doctrinal support for church on Sunday versus church on Saturday. We also use this in support of the collections we take on Sunday.

We find one only scripture in the entire New Testament about Sunday collections. 1 Corinthians 16:1 and 2, "Now concerning the collection for the saints, as I have given order to the churches of Galatia, even so do ye. Upon the first day of the week let every one of you lay by him in store, as God hath prospered him, that there be no gatherings when I come."

This particular directive was to give to bless and uphold the needy saints in Jerusalem. They were to collect the offerings on Sunday, and over a period of time, accumulate the resulting finances. Paul would be there at a later time and gather the moneys raised by a number of churches, and see that these funds got to Jerusalem to bless the saints. This means the needy people in the church of Jerusalem.

This Sunday offering was taught by Paul to all churches. This Sunday offering was termed the collection for the saints. *What? For the saints? Did the saints get it?* We need to research this. Do you and I get it? This was not for the needy ministry, apostles and elders.

Another text possibly referring to ministry finances, although it does not explicitly say so, is 1 Timothy 5:17, which says an elder who labors in the word is worthy of "double honor." The only other scripture I could find in the New Testament honoring the ministries right to financial support is Acts 6:2, which does not address ministry finances specifically. There it says to let others attend to tables, while the apostles attend to the word and prayer. Let us study this subject prayerfully.

2 Corinthians 9: 6 through 12, "But this I say, He which soweth sparingly shall reap also sparingly; and he which soweth bountifully shall reap also bountifully. He hath dispersed abroad; he hath given to the poor. Now he that ministereth seed to the sower both minister bread for your food, and multiply your seed sown, and increase the fruits of your righteousness; Being enriched in every thing to all bountifulness, which causeth through us thanksgiving to God. For the administration of this service not only supplieth the want of the saints, but is abundant also by many thanksgivings unto God."

Many times I have heard the pre-offering sermonette include this scripture about sowing and reaping. The purpose is to encourage believers to enter into a faith realm, causing them to give bountifully and trust God to bless them in reaping, based on their faithful giving. Tremendous truth! God will bless those who enter into a covenant with God, to give faithfully and cheerfully as He leads them to.

Never have I read this presented with the intent of verse nine, that this giving is sowing to supply for the poor. I have never heard this presented as verse twelve states, to "supply the want of the saints."

The heart beat behind most presentations is to supply anything but the wants of the saints. Hello! No matter what your views are on finances and needs, let us use and not abuse this scripture, by presenting it fully and in context. *Shocking is it not?* Teachings and scriptures about collections for the poor and the needy saint, are used to entice giving to the poor minister in charge and church practical needs. Even if half the proceeds went to the pastor and practical issues, and half went to the needs of the saint and poor, there would be some semblance of correct usage of scripture. Usually less than one percent of that amount is used for the poor saints' needs.

Offerings and Giving

The disciples gathered together on the first day of the week, celebrated communion, (broke bread) and gave their offerings, not tithes (1 Cor. 16:1-2).

Financial giving was termed "your liberality, collections, gatherings and offerings," but never tithes in the New Testament. Why? Because tithing was part of the law, along with the animal sacrifices, and the other "Thou shalts." Christ died and fulfilled the law for righteousness, and tithing as a law ended with it. We are now under the law of the Spirit, and give under this law as the Lord speaks to our hearts.

The only law that stands in the New Testament era is the ten commandments. Jesus said that He had not come to do away with the law, but to fulfill it (Math. 5:17). The ten commandments were epitomized with two commandments, "Thou shalt love the Lord with all of your heart, and thy neighbor as yourself" (Mark 12:30). The only law of the ten that is not kept the same way is the Sabbath law. We worship on the first day of the week, or the eight day instead of the seventh day. This is because of the scriptural New Testament examples, and because the number of Jesus Christ is eight. The eighth day is the day of new beginnings, His Kingdom and Lordship (Acts 2:35, Rom. 5:21,Phil. 3:5, circumcision 8th day, Dan. 2:44, etc.). All other laws were ceremonial (Heb.9:1-10).

I believe in the principle of tithing, the giving of ten to thirty two percent, instead of the "law" of tithing. What is the difference, if the base percentage of giving is the same? Namely, if one received anything under the tithe law system in the Old Testament, they were to tithe from it, or give ten percent. This included crops and other things as well as money. If they did not tithe accurately, they were in sin. In the New Testament after the death of Christ, we are under the law of the Spirit. This came with the new covenant spoken of in Jeremiah 31:31 and Hebrews 8:10. God said He would put His laws within our hearts and minds.

The affect of this is a living walk with greater responsibility. We now need to make moral decisions about giving, and not just follow a rule of behavior. In 2 Corinthians 8:12, it says, "*For if there be first a willing mind, it is accepted according to that a man hath, and not according to that he hath not."* This totally different from the law of tithing. This applies to the single mom who just barely manages to pay her bills with no room in her budget to give anything. If she is enticed to breach the scripture "Owe no man anything," and encouraged to tithe, and then owes someone as a result, she is acting out of a teaching of the law. This scripture allows for grace; God looks upon the heart and accepts this person who wanted to give and could not. Rather than challenging saints like this into presumptuous giving under the pretext of faith and laying a false guilt trip on them, give to them! This in no wise takes away from the righteous challenge to people to give when they can, and expect a blessing. THE DISTINCTION MADE IS IMPORTANT!

Tithing under the law was a righteous, proper, and acceptable amount, since the amount was set by our holy and righteous God. We do well to consider this as a benchmark for giving, but not a law. The principle of tithing was acknowledged in righteousness, some four hundred years before the law was given (Gal. 3:17). Abraham and Jacob understood the blessing of tithing, long before the laws of tithing were given to and through Moses. The principle of tithing and giving to God, and expecting His faithful blessing, is just and fair after the law is done away with as well. However, we must not teach a legalistic tithing. Consider David taking and eating the shewbread, and Jesus healing people on the Sabbath. They were acting out a greater law which we who walk after the Spirit should understand.

This law word *tithe* does not appear after Christ. Instead it says in 1 Corinthians 16:2, "Upon the first day of the week let every one of you lay by him in store, as God hath prospered him." May we apply this as we teach people to give. May we teach (1 Tim. 1:9) that even the ten commandments are not for righteous men, who walk after the Spirit, and do not fulfill the lusts of the flesh (Rom. 8:4).

Acts 20:7, "And upon the first day of the week, when the disciples came together to break bread, Paul preached unto them, ready to depart on the morrow..."

1 Corinthians 16:1 to 2, "Now concerning the collection for the saints, as I have given order to the churches of Galatia, even so do ye. Upon the first day of the week let every one of you lay

by him in store, as God hath prospered him, that there be no gatherings when I come."

On Sunday, give unto the Lord according to God's prospering of your person. May we faithfully give as unto the Lord, and He will supply all of our needs.

We are commanded to be diligent and supply our own needs. We are to be an example to those without and be virtuous in our finances. By doing so, we will not lack. However, if we do, may the brethren and church help in the hour of need! 1 Thessalonians 4:11 and 12, "And that ye study to be quiet, and to do your own business, and to work with your own hands, as we commanded you; That ye may walk honestly toward them that are without, and that ye may have lack of nothing."

2 Corinthians 9:12, "For the administration of this service not only supplieth the want of the saints, but is abundant also by many thanksgivings unto God."

May a hallelujah be heard in heaven when the saints who are the needful recipients of this offering worship God for His mercy. May the giving church give upon receiving the offerings and cause this thankfulness. May we remember the poor.

The normal church in the New Testament gave constantly to other needy churches, to care for the saints. Today this practice is practically eliminated.

• In Acts 4:34. and 35, distribution was made unto every man.

• In 2 Corinthians 8:1 and 2, Corinth gave to the Macedonian poor.

• Acts 11:29 we see the Antioch church giving to the needy in the Judea churches.

This is the consistent picture. People were challenged to give, and tithing amounts were a bare minimum.

If we truly walk after the Spirit and listen for His voice, we may be challenged to give more than ten percent in many cases. We will give according to needs and the leading of the Holy Spirit within. Some were challenged to give a new car or house to be used for ministry purposes, well beyond any ten percent giving. However, if you struggle with Holy Spirit-led giving, which is usually more than ten percent, give what God set in the Old Testament as an acceptable norm and you will be blessed. God only receives free-will offerings and not tithes that are required. This was exemplified in the building of the tabernacle and the temple, where God met with man. God will never meet with man out of duty or in a house established by duty. Just remember as you give by faith that you will never outgive God.

Church Distribution of Offerings and Finances

We will get to the topic of giving to ministries, but let us first review the scriptural teachings on collections and distribution of money. Churches in the New Testament had a genuine care one for another, which went as deep as their wallet, and that is truly an act of God (Acts 4:32-37)!

As previously noted, in 1 Corinthians 16:1 the churches of Galatia, Corinth and others were told to take up their collections on the first day of the week (Sunday). These collections were for the saints in Jerusalem. The saints in Jerusalem were having difficulties, as discussed in 2 Corinthians 8:10-15. Paul reminded them that their liberality was not to just provide others with a free ride, but bring about equality. Again, in verse 16 he states that *this service supplied the wants of the saints.*

This caring for members in others churches with needs conforms with the law of love. Powerful! This could very well include ministers and elders who are also saints. May they act saintly in finances. When the Jerusalem apostles blessed Paul and Barnabas and sent them on their way, they gave them only two commandments (Gal. 2:10). One of these was "remember the poor." Today this is practically interpreted as the poor pastor, singular. After this need is looked after and some overhead taken care of, in most cases there is no money left for the saints. Praise God there are some exceptions, but they are few. We have drifted far from the New Testament example, and the "love of the root of all evil" has taken over (1 Tim. 6:10). With proper structure in leadership and understanding in finances this can be reversed. When we do manage to reverse it, we may even see the anointing demonstrated in the early church and thousands added daily.

In Romans 15:25 to 27, we again read about this same topic. "But now I go unto Jerusalem to minister unto the saints. For it hath pleased them of Macedonia and Achaia to make a certain contribution for the poor saints which are at Jerusalem. It hath pleased them verily; and their debtors they are. For if the Gentiles have been made partakers of their spiritual things, their duty is also to minister unto them in carnal things." They are reminded of their debt, spiritually speaking, to the more mature spiritual "source church." This needs to be addressed today.

The ministry to the poor involves the genuine reinstatement of the holy office of deacon. This involves ministry to the widows and orphans financially. Today we push them to the State welfare program, or do not touch this area of their lives. Proper ministry addresses their needs within the congregation. Deacons can dispense aid along with wisdom, righteous judgment, and teaching on finances, financial responsibility, and holy living (Acts 6:1). Today we see more of what was warned about in three separate gospels, including Matthew 23:14, where Pharisees devour widows houses for a prayer, instead of blessing their lives with care. You can push widows under the law of tithing, and refuse speak to them through the appropriate ministry about their personal welfare, but you should not wonder why you are experiencing spiritual drought (Isai. 58:1-10).

Eldership and Ministries Working

Let's look at numerous scriptural examples set out in the New Testament, and draw some conclusions.

First, it was normal for apostles to work with their own hands.

•1 Cor. 4:11 through 16, "Even unto this present hour we both hunger, and thirst, and are naked, and are buffeted, and have no certain dwelling place; *And labor, working with our own hands:* being reviled, we bless; being persecuted, we suffer it: Being defamed, we intreat: we are made as the filth of the world, and are the offscouring of all things unto this day. I write not these things to shame you, but as my beloved sons I warn you. For though ye have ten thousand instructors in Christ, yet have ye not many fathers: for in Christ Jesus I have begotten you through the gospel. Wherefore I beseech you, be ye followers of me."

•2 Cor. 11:7, 8 and 9, "Have I committed an offense in abasing myself that ye might be exalted, because I have preached to you the gospel of God freely? I robbed other churches, taking wages of them, to do you service. And when I was present with you, and wanted, *I was chargeable to no man:* for that which was lacking to me the brethren which came from Macedonia supplied: and in all things I have kept myself from being burdensome unto you, and so will I keep myself."

Paul determined not to take money from this church while he ministered among them. He did receive support and love offerings from other churches. He spoke of his determined stance not to take finances from this Corinthian church. Then he goes on to point out a further step and stronger truth in 2 Corinthians 11:18 to 20. "Seeing that many glory after the flesh, I will glory also. For ye suffer fools gladly, seeing ye yourselves are wise. For ye suffer, if a man bring you into bondage, if a man devour you, if a man take of you, if a man exalt himself, if a man smite you on the face."

WOW! He calls them fools when they allow others to take money from them. He says that in fact those that do this exalt themselves, slap them in the face, and devour them. Have you heard this Bible text or any of the several like it preached lately? Ever? Why not? These scriptures differ with our teachings of today, and we have departed from the scriptural pattern a long way. These, people of God, are God's words and not mine. We do not see this teaching in today's church, along with those who preach the gospel rights.

Second, IT WAS NORMAL FOR ALL MINISTERS AND ELDERS TO WORK, AND THE APOSTLES GAVE THE EXAMPLE. IT WAS NEVER INTENDED THAT PASTORS OR ANY OTHER MINISTRY GET A FREE RIDE.

ALSO, SHOULD THERE BE FINANCES AVAILABLE AFTER CONSIDERING THE POOR, MAY THERE BE EQUITY AND IMPARTIALITY. Why should pastors get a salary, and all other ministries and elders scrounge with hand-offs (Acts 20:34)?

Receive the teaching of this scripture admonishing the elders to follow Paul's example, to labor with their hands to supply the needs of the poor first. This is not to say that it is always wrong for a minister to receive financial support. There are times when it is expedient for some ministers to tend to the Word and ministry affairs. It is wrong when this is clutched onto as a way of life. It is wrong when a few, who choose to deny and ignore their fellow ministers and elders, hoard financial control, attempt to justify themselves scripturally, and deny the call of God in their fellow elder. They totally or almost totally ignore the poor and needy. More important, you ignore and deny Jesus Christ when you deny your fellow elder. You deny the call and appointment of God in your brother or sister, and thereby ignore God himself! You rob the church of the banquet table God intended for the saints. You have been and are proud and puffed up, with your self worth, proven by not seeking out and dealing with equality of your brethren! In a word, REPENT!

2 Corinthians 12:15 through 18, "And I will very gladly spend and be spent for you; though the more abundantly I love you, the less I be loved. But be it so, I did not burden you: nevertheless, being crafty, I caught you with guile. Did I make a gain of you by any of them whom I sent unto you? I desired Titus, and with him I sent a brother. Did Titus make a gain of you? walked we not in the same spirit? walked we not in the same steps?"

Walked we not in the same spirit? May we see the heart of Christ in this statement. A giving heart does not want to put a burden on the people of God, unless we deem them to be strong. This was not only Paul's heart, but the heart of Titus and any ministers associated with Paul as well. This was his teaching to elders and ministers, made elders and ministers by the Holy Ghost. Lord, help us! (Acts 20:28)

2 Thessalonians 3:7 to 10, "For yourselves know how ye ought to follow us: for we behaved not ourselves disorderly among you; Neither did we eat any man's bread for naught; but wrought with labor and travail night and day, that we might not be chargeable to any of you: Not because we have not power, BUT TO MAKE OURSELVES AN EXAMPLE UNTO YOU, TO FOLLOW US. For even when we were with you, this we commanded you, that if any would not work, neither should he eat."

This teaching was given to the Thessalonian church. Again Paul points out that this work ethic was not applied because he did not have the right to expect material and financial support from them. Rather, this was a consistent decision of living out a higher and better way, thereby being an example to the leadership, according to the law of love! He also points out each person's responsibility to eat when he earns his way. Consider Acts 20: 34 and 35, "Yea, ye yourselves know, that *these hands have ministered unto my necessities, and to them that were with me.* I have showed you all things, how that so laboring ye ought to support the weak" *(ministers supporting the weak).*

1 Corinthians 9: 18, "What is my reward then? Verily that, when I preach the gospel, I may make the gospel of Christ without charge, that I abuse not my power in the gospel."

Paul said that making the gospel available and preaching the gospel without charge was his privilege. Jesus said, "No man takes my life from me, but I lay it down." Paul also said in Second Corinthians 12:14 that it is proper for the parents to supply for the children. A true father's heart mirrors the heart of the Father, our Lord.

I Thessalonians 2:5 through 10, "For neither at any time used we flattering words, as ye know, nor a cloak of covetousness; God is witness: Nor of men sought we glory, neither of you, nor yet of others, when we might have been burdensome, as the apostles of Christ. But we were gentle among you, even as a nurse cherisheth her children: So being affectionately desirous of you, we were willing to have imparted unto you, not the gospel of God only, but also our own souls, because ye were dear unto us. For ye remember, brethren, our labor and travail: *for laboring night and day, because we would not be chargeable unto any of you, we preached unto you the gospel of God. Ye are witnesses, and God also, how holy and justly and unblameably we behaved ourselves among you.*"

Paul considered it holy and just behavior to work and earn his own way while ministering to this church. It was an act of holy benevolence. He considered this act of caring for them as unblameable behavior and left no doubt in any man's mind that he was not covetous of their goods. He clearly pointed out that he had the authority to partake of their support financially, yet with a holy focus, determined not to.

Acts 18:3 and 4, "And because he was of the same craft, he abode with them, and wrought: for by their occupation they were tentmakers. And he reasoned in the synagogue every Sabbath, and persuaded the Jews and the Greeks."

Here we see the practical side of this matter. Paul may have been a Pharisee, and studied at the feet of Gamaliel (Acts 22:3), but he also learned a practical trade along the way. He abode with people of a like trade to facilitate his earning ability and "wrought." He planned his stay among them, and this plan included not making himself burdensome. While he physically worked there, did he have less of a place of ministry among them? Of course not! Was he still the elder brother who was correct in his assessment of himself when he said you do not have many fathers? Of course he was. Did he temporarily lose or give up his spiritual authority because he got his hands dirty working on tents, with skins and physical things? No!

As the Lord Jesus spent time training twelve plus men during his three year ministry, Paul spent three years in this church being an example to the ministry and eldership. At the end of it all, he told them to follow his example of working with their hands to bless the church. So minister to the poor and weak. Not just the word ministry, but practical, caring, giving, genuine ministry.

Needful Scriptures

• Rom. 12:12, "Rejoicing in hope; patient in tribulation; continuing instant in prayer; Distributing to the necessity of saints; given to hospitality."

• Galatians 6:10, "As we have therefore opportunity, let us do good unto all men, especially unto them who are of the household of faith."

• Ephesians 4:28, "Let him that stole steal no more: but rather let him labor, working with his hands the thing which is good, that he may have to give to him that needeth."

• 1 Timothy 6:17 to 18, "Charge them that are rich in this world, That they do good, that they be rich in good works, ready to distribute, willing to communicate."

• Galatians 2:10, "Only they would that we should remember the poor; the same which I also was forward to do." (The only commandment given by the Jerusalem apostles except to abstain from blood).

• 1 Timothy 5:3, "Honor widows that are widows indeed." (May we hear this one.)

Attitude to Finances

2 Corinthians 9:6 to 8, "But this I say, He which soweth sparingly shall reap also sparingly; and he which soweth bountifully shall reap also bountifully. Every man according as he purposeth in his heart, so let him give; not grudgingly, or of necessity: for God loveth a cheerful giver. And God is able to make all grace abound toward you."

We read how we should give, and this has nothing to do with tithing. Let every man give as he purposes in his heart. Give cheerfully for God loves a cheerful giving person. Give (sow) much and expect to reap much. May we find the grace to live a life of giving. May we have the wisdom where to give. May we know when not to give. May we give unto the Lord, with joy!

2 Corinthians 9:10 to 11, "Now he that ministereth seed to the sower both minister bread for your food, and multiply your seed sown, and increase the fruits of your righteousness; Being enriched in every thing to all bountifulness, which causeth through us thanksgiving to God. For the administration of this service not only *supplieth the want of the saints*, but is abundant also by many thanksgivings unto God."

Our giving meets the needs of the saints and causes them to bless God and worship Him. The financial ministry to the saints, helping them in their needs, is sowing in God's garden. A crop will surely come up in every area of our lives when our motives are clean and holy.

1 Thessalonians 4:12, "That ye may walk honestly toward them that are without, and that ye may have lack of nothing."

We need to see our Godly responsibility to be diligent in the work arena. So shall the world see our Godliness. We need to be very careful financially, since we are epistles seen and read of all men. By working diligently, we are to supply our needs and the needs of those given to us, as well as the needs of the less fortunate and capable in the church and family of God.

2 Thessalonians 3:10 to 14, "For even when we were with you, this we commanded you, that if any would not work, neither

should he eat. For we hear that there are some which walk among you disorderly, working not at all, but are busybodies. Now them that are such we command and exhort by our Lord Jesus Christ, that with quietness they work, and eat their own bread. But ye, brethren, be not weary in well doing. And if any man obey not our word by this epistle, note that man, and have no company with him, that he may be ashamed."

Living "By Faith," Foolishness, or Presumption

Perhaps this should be applied to those who are "living by faith." I ask you, faith in what? You never learned a doing nothing attitude from the scriptures. Paul and ministries associated with him never headed in this direction of waiting on God for someone to give to them while the less spiritual and ignorant souls worked to supply for them. Rather, he worked to care for the less spiritually mature and ignorant as well as himself, and taught this as an example to ministers. Those who do not work should not eat. A beautiful Christian brother rented his house to a "spiritual" couple, who robbed him of a half a year's rent, while saying they were not to move because the Lord had not directed them yet. One day the Lord directed them. He told them to move through this same brother who was tired of their supposedly spiritual walk and being robbed by the devil. He realized that these two were not making every effort to better their circumstances, and that he was enabling them to live an ungodly life style.

1 Timothy 5:8, "But if any provide not for his own, and specially for those of his own house, he hath denied the faith, and is worse than an infidel."

Perhaps when you as a ministry see your family suffer, and when you have gotten into the bad habit of beating up the sheep for your support, you should consider this scripture and take on some secular work to support yourself and give to others.

Perhaps when you in the ministry see another person who rightfully is an elder/minister denied any financial help while you grab all income available, you will think on these scriptures. Consider getting some kind of work to support yourself at least partially. Whatever you do, do not consider this to be lack of faith, but as worship unto our lord. John the beloved did say, "by love serve one another" (1 Jn. 4:7-8).

The church is to help the poor. Part of the help is to teach them work ethics, and their responsibility to make every effort on their own behalf. When they hold out their hands for help, and refuse teaching and Godly counsel, treat them as infidels and not believers. If they buy their own ticket, let them take the ride. Tough love is genuine love. Do not enable them to live in sin.

1 Timothy 6:10 and 11, "For the love of money is the root of all evil: which while some coveted after, they have erred from the faith, and pierced themselves through with many sorrows. But thou, O man of God, flee these things; and follow after righteousness."

Did you see what righteousness meant, as Paul taught Timothy in financial matters?

Lord, may we despise evil, and the love of money. May we not covet money, yet be diligent and see the true value of money, as a means to an end. You are our source of goods, and Jehovah Jireh is Your name. We rejoice in you and not strength, wisdom or riches.

1 Peter 5:1 and 2, "The elders which are among you I exhort, who am also an elder, and a witness of the sufferings of Christ, and also a partaker of the glory that shall be revealed: Feed the flock of God which is among you, taking the oversight thereof, not by constraint, but willingly; not for filthy lucre."

May we minister because of our love of Christ, and love for the people, and shun the financial aspects as a motive for ministering anywhere.

1 Corinthians 9:18, "What is my reward then? Verily that, when I preach the gospel, I may make the gospel of Christ without charge, that I abuse not my power in the gospel."

Paul had every right to financial support. That was within his power, yet he did not demand or want to exercise this right. His reward was to be able to preach the gospel without charge. Are we less spiritual if we follow him in this course? When filling out ministerial papers from year to year, I always struggle with the question of "Do you minister full-time, or do you work as well?" The call of God is on the person called to the ministry, regardless of working or not working. When we work and minister, we are serving the Lord and people in His name, and possibly are closer to the unpreached scriptural examples cited. Help us, Lord. In 2 Peter 2:1-3, Paul speaks of those who with feigned words make merchandise of you. *Beware! Especially of those who demand their financial rights, ignore both the poor and their fellow elders and ministries, and do not make practical, apostle-led world ministry vision a priority!*

Sharing Church Finances

Acts 4:31-32, "And when they had prayed, the place was shaken where they were assembled together; and they were all filled with the Holy Ghost, and they spake the word of God with boldness. And the multitude of them that believed were of one heart and of one soul: neither said any of them that ought of the things which he possessed was his own; but they had all things common."

Most of us want the Holy Ghost to shake the place. Are we also ready to usher in the Holy Ghost with our financial course and habits? The Holy Ghost will make us of "one soul." This will change the financial views and dealings of all. Why not do the change, and usher in the Holy Ghost!

Acts 6:1, "And in those days, when the number of the disciples was multiplied, there arose a murmuring of the Grecians against the Hebrews, because their widows were neglected in the daily ministration. Then the twelve called the multitude of the disciples unto them, and said, It is not reason that we should leave the word of God, and serve tables. Wherefore, brethren, look ye out among you seven men of honest report, full of the Holy Ghost and wisdom, whom we may appoint over this business."

How do you rate? Dare you take the test? Do those widows, bruised, and fatherless exist? In your church? Have you cared for them? Maybe we pay taxes and the state should look after them? *Lord Jesus! Have mercy!*

Acts 11:28, "And there stood up one of them named Agabus, and signified by the Spirit that there should be great dearth throughout all the world: which came to pass in the days of Claudius Caesar. Then the disciples, every man according to his ability, determined to send relief unto the brethren which dwelt in Judea." No tithes here, just heart. A heart for God! A heart for the saints. Not even in *our* church, but *the* church.

Galatians 2:10, "ONLY, they would that we should remember the poor; the same which I also was forward to do."

1 Corinthians 13:1, Though I speak with the tongues of men and of angels; Though I am a great preacher; Though I teach many people; Though I have the fastest growing church in my area; and have not charity, I am become as sounding brass, or a tinkling cymbal. Hello!

Philippians 2:4, "Look not every man on his own things, but every man also on the things of others."

1 Timothy 5:8 to 10 and 16, "But if any provide not for his own, and specially for those of his own house, he hath denied the faith, and is worse than an infidel. Let not a widow be taken into the number under threescore years old, having been the wife of one man, Well reported of for good works; If any man or woman that believeth have widows, let them relieve them, and let not the church be charged; that it may relieve them that are widows indeed."

May we discern where and when to take responsibility for people, and our responsibility to provide. I have heard some horror stories of pastors beating up the sheep over finances, and never considering the possibility of anything less than their right. These men never considered the possibility of working and providing finances for the poor sheep.

1 Timothy 6:17, "Charge them that are rich in this world, that they be not high-minded, nor trust in uncertain riches, but in the living God, who giveth us richly all things to enjoy; That they do good, that they be rich in good works, ready to distribute, willing to communicate."

"Charity suffereth long, is kind; charity vaunteth not itself, doth not behave itself unseemly, *seeketh not her own*, but rejoiceth in the truth."

Church Support, Ministries, and Apostles

Acts 4:33 to 37, "And with great power gave the apostles witness of the resurrection of the Lord Jesus: and great grace was upon them all. Neither was there any among them that lacked: for as many as were possessors of lands or houses sold them, and brought the prices of the things that were sold, And laid them down at the apostles' feet: and distribution was made unto every man according as he had need. And Joses, who by the apostles was surnamed Barnabas, which is, being interpreted, The son of consolation, a Levite, and of the country of Cyprus, Having land, sold it, and brought the money, and laid it at the apostles' feet."

Here we have the financial facts and accounting at the beginning of the first century church. The setting was dynamic, as the Holy Spirit had just been poured out with an awesome demonstration of the supernatural. The continued witness of the resurrection of the Lord Jesus was demonstrated by the Holy Spirit gifts operating through the apostles. Hearts were turned to God with a fresh bath of love. This Holy Ghost love permeated the believers to such a degree that their love for the brethren showed in their spontaneous actions. Finances flowed in for the cares and needs of the people so that no lack was mentioned. *The apostles were the orchestrators of financial affairs.* Those who acted in hypocrisy were dealt with in that rarefied air of holiness (chapter 5).

The first problem mentioned in the church ministry was the lack in the care of widows, and immediately, under Holy Ghost direction, the apostles acted. Deacons were set in place to address the care of those who needed help with material things. This is our example and the New Testament pattern. Later this was refined as the church grew. Instructions about dealing with loafers and lazy free riders were given out (1 Tim. 5:8). The care of widows was qualified by qualifying the widows, but the financial care for the needy saints was consistent throughout the entire New Testament.

Today, many will set a great priority on building a beautiful temple, and little on the care and building of the true temple, the saints. May the apostles be identified and allowed to set things in order again, including the financial affairs of the church.

1 Corinthians 16:1 to 6, "Now concerning the collection for the saints, And when I come, whomsoever ye shall approve by your letters, them will I send to bring your liberality unto Jerusalem. And if it be meet that I go also, they shall go with me. Now I will come unto you, when I shall pass through Macedonia:

for I do pass through Macedonia. And it may be that I will abide, yea, and winter with you, that ye may bring me on my journey."

The topic was financial blessings for the poor saints in Jerusalem. Paul also told the Corinthian church that he intended to stay with them over the winter. In other writings he clearly stated that he never took any thing from them during his stay with them, but labored with his hands to bless them (1 Cor. 4:10). The one thing he did expect was for them to "bring him on his way" to the next destination. In other words, *he told them boldly of his desire to have them pay his travel expenses.* He did not even ask them if they would, but he presumed on them in this regard, as his right. Here we have a clear picture of the apostle ministry. He gave them the gospel freely, and would not take anything from them when he ministered among them, but here exercised his authority rights in this regard. He also declared this to be their reasonable responsibility under God.

2 Corinthians 1:11, "Ye also helping together by prayer for us, that for the gift bestowed upon us by the means of many persons thanks may be given by many on our behalf."

Verse 16, "And to pass by you into Macedonia, and to come again out of Macedonia unto you, and of you to be brought on my way toward Judea."

Again we see this topic addressed more fully. He had a bag full of money in his possession, to give to the poor saints in Jerusalem (1 Cor. 16:3). He did not touch this as it was a holy trust in his care.

Instead he worked as he ministered among them, even knowing his rights to financial support (1 Cor. 9:6). He specifically stated (verse 19), "I abuse not my power in the gospel." How could he abuse his power in the gospel, when he just finished saying "they which preach the gospel should live of the gospel"? He understood the law of love! He did not want to put weight on them. He treated them as a baby church, probably seeing newly saved people added on a regular basis. He taught ministers to follow his example. He was the father elder, and they were the children (2 Cor. 12:14). All ministries involved with him also had this attitude (2 Cor. 12:18).

However, when it came to receiving financial help, there were two things he received, and one of those two things he insisted on. First, he received a love gift from time to time, and thanked them for it. This was usually given as a ministry support while he was ministering and building up other church works (Phil. 4:15-18). While he was in Thessalonica, the Philippian church blessed Paul with a love offering several times, and here in 2 Corinthians 1:11, Paul thanked the Corinthian church for their love gift which he received while ministering elsewhere.

THE SECOND financial help he insisted on and received was finances to forward his mission work and gospel travels. This is the consistent New testament teaching.

Romans 15:24, "Whenever I take my journey into Spain, I will come to you: for I trust to see you in my journey, and to be brought on my way there by you, if first I be somewhat filled with your company." Rome, I expect you to bring me on my journey to Spain.

This was Paul's normal financial stance. We need to make sure finances are available for the foundation ministries' planting and building. If some salaried ministries consume all the available church funds, without the flow of the multiple ministry, support of the poor, support of the apostle and traveling planting ministries, we are outside of the scriptural pattern.

2 Corinthians 11:7 and following verses, "But we have been thoroughly made manifest among you in all things. Have I committed an offense in abasing myself that ye might be exalted, because I have preached to you the gospel of God freely? I robbed other churches, taking wages of them, to do you service. And when I was present with you, and wanted, I was chargeable to no man: for that which was lacking to me the brethren which came from Macedonia supplied: and in all things I have kept myself from being burdensome unto you, and so will I keep myself. As the truth of Christ is in me, no man shall stop me of this boasting in the regions of Achaia."

Here we see the heart of the matter, and the financial system employed. The word of God is clear.

2 Corinthians 11:12 and 13, *"But what I do, that I will do,* that I may cut off occasion from them which desire occasion; *that wherein they glory, they may be found even as we.* For such are false apostles, deceitful workers, transforming themselves into the apostles of Christ."

Here Paul addresses his motive, and teaches that other ministries ought to follow his example. No doubt someone will say, "perhaps this is just for apostles." These same people will not deal with Acts 20:34. Some will reason this was only for the Ephesian church, but we find the same example in the Corinthian church, and all the churches in the region of Achaia (2 Cor. 11:7-10). Some will say this applied to the baby churches. Paul spent several years in Corinth, which was an established church. He left an example, and pointing out that others he sent to them over a period of time also gave this example. *He spent three years with the Ephesian church (Acts 20:31), and stated his example was meant to teach them to continuously serve the weak by laboring and raising finances to support them in some manner.*

Some will argue the pastors are not elders, even though the elders led the church everywhere in the New Testament. To do so would be taking the position that none were present in Ephesus, since they all came. Some might debate that pastors were not in submission to apostles—as very few are today— but this would be denying 1 Corinthians 12:18, and many more scriptures. Some will attempt to find some argument, simply because they will not conform to scriptural precedent and need to justify themselves. They will not yield to the Lordship of Christ. Lord, have mercy on them!

Philippians 2:29, "Receive him therefore in the Lord with all gladness; and hold such in reputation: Because for the work of Christ he was nigh unto death, not regarding his life, to supply your lack of service toward me."

This lack of service was in *not upholding the apostle in his world vision ministry, and limiting Christ by not allowing this gospel to flow into all the world.* This is prevalent today.

Philippians 4:10 through 16, "But I rejoiced in the Lord greatly, that now at the last your care of me hath flourished again; wherein ye were also careful, but ye lacked opportunity. Not that I speak in respect of want: for I have learned, in whatsoever state I am, therewith to be content. I know both how to be abased, and I know how to abound: every where and in all things I am instructed both to be full and to be hungry, both to abound and to suffer need. I can do all things through Christ which strengtheneth me. Notwithstanding ye have well done, that ye did communicate with my affliction. Now ye Philippians know also, that in the beginning of the gospel, when I departed from Macedonia, no church communicated with me as concerning giving and receiving, but ye only. For even in Thessalonica ye sent once and again unto my necessity."

We need to uphold apostles in their vision. The true apostle will then uphold the prophet and all ministries in their vision. May our love for Christ and the church continue. May our love for the brethren continue (Heb. 13:1).

3 John 1 to 8, "The elder unto the well beloved Gaius, whom I love in the truth. Beloved, I wish above all things that thou mayest prosper and be in health, even as thy soul prospereth. For I rejoiced greatly, when the brethren came and testified of the truth that is in thee, even as thou walkest in the truth. I have no greater joy than to hear that my children walk in truth. Beloved, thou doest faithfully whatsoever thou doest to the brethren, AND TO STRANGERS; Which have borne witness of thy charity before the church: whom if thou bring forward on their journey after a godly sort, thou shalt do well: Because that for his name's sake they went forth, taking nothing of the Gentiles. We therefore ought to receive such, that we might be fellow helpers to the truth."

Lord, help us to read and receive this scripture in our spirits. When I and many others go overseas, we can not take from the churches we go to plant and encourage. Sometimes we receive a love offering from them ,which usually amounts to very little in terms of U.S. funds. We do receive these as an expression of their love for us and to encourage their giving. In my experience, the amount involved does very little to support our ministry. Instead, we take finances to give as the Lord leads us, when we are able to do so.

Receive strangers who are used of God to proclaim the gospel to others, of whom they will take nothing. Love, pure love. Them and us. May we discern stranger ministries, and bless them on their way. I remember a Filipino minister who came to our area in Canada while I was pastoring a small church. He was brought over by a brother with a big heart to teach a YWAM team heading for the Philippines. He had nowhere to preach or receive an honorarium. Someone brought him to our Wednesday evening fellowship group, where I gave him the floor. At the end of the evening, I casually mentioned to people to remember this brother. An offering of over four hundred dollars was given, and when I gave it to this brother, the anointing came down.

Philippians 3:17, "Brethren, be followers together of me, and mark them which walk so as ye have us for an ensample."

This is the scriptural norm. May we obey the examples set before us. Study the scriptures in regard to all financial dealings and examples given to us. Now follow them! If we do, and apply this to any traveling ministries, especially apostles, prophets, evangelists and teachers from time to time, the affect will be awesome. If this is practiced according to scriptural norms, the gospel will reach this world in a very short time. Yes, we do need to discern clean ministries, and yes, there may be some abuse, but let us prayerfully follow the examples given to us in the word.

Imagine if all churches had working elders as was portrayed in Acts 20:35, and besides looking after the needs of the poor and needy (Gal. 2:10), they gave financial priority to assisting ministries who would go into all the world. Matthew 28:19 would be fulfilled in short time. Apply half of the home church ministry giving to direct mission and church planting with the correct ministries in charge and flowing with an apostolic order, and millions of people will be swept into the kingdom. The saints and churches would be established! The heart of our God, who wills that none should perish, would rejoice (2 Pet. 3:9).

As long as the home ministry eats the home granary like mice unchecked, and leaves no room for this scriptural pattern and example, the WORLD gospel outreach will stagnate.

May the financial structure allow all the ministries to function. Why should one ministry get a salary, and others work? These other ministries are being despised. The one receiving the financial benefits is not esteeming others better than self, and not acknowledging his need for others.

Should the church work truly demand the full-time efforts of several ministries, it is scriptural to let the ministries attend to ministry. In Acts 6:2, the first apostles were engulfed in a major church explosion, and it was not reasonable for them to serve at tables; it was only reasonable for them to attend to the Word and prayer. This was a temporary necessity. Later when Paul visited

the Jerusalem church, the majority of these apostles were gone
(Gal. 1:18). We also see repetition of the terms *apostles* and *elders*
in several chapters in the book of Acts. We need to apply wisdom
to implement the scriptural pattern, but never the less, do it. May
we desire to see the financial structure implemented in such a
way that Acts 20:35 will be embraced as a holy directive. May we
see Ephesians 4:11 become a reality.

Parachurch?

Many Christian organizations flow outside an understood
church group. These are upheld by believers, who prayerfully
and financially bless them in their efforts. Praise God for the
vision that they operate under, and those who send in offerings
to enable them. Some are led by apostles, prophets, teachers, and
evangelists.

Jesus said those who are not against us are for us. They are
the church, not "parachurch." They should all flow with a church
body and multiple ministry. Most would if the churches allowed
them to or understood these ministries, who usually do not have
a pastor calling. We need to understand and discern all ministries, and flow with them within the scriptural five-fold ministry
callings. Allowed them to function with their God given unction.
Remember that ministry to the church is team play. They are the
eyes, arms, legs and mouths of our Lord Jesus Christ.

One example is the 700 Club. I have never met Pat Robertson,
but I greatly respect the work of his ministry. Their group is
reaching millions of people with the gospel in tangible ways.
There are many smaller groups doing an effective work for the
Kingdom of God. These can call on the people of God to support
their efforts. May the Lord help all of them to be faithful in their
stewardship. They are reaching the world.

A smaller but effective ministry in Canada is Prayer Canada.
The prophet ministry who leads it has spread intercessory prayer
groups called "Prayer Posts" all across Canada. These are made
up of interdenominational believers, who intercede for the nation.
Many meet in the council chambers of the highest offices of
government, one hour a week, to act out 2 Chronicles 7:14. Who
can measure the value of such a ministry on the scales of eternity?

These ministries are acting out the call of God placed within them. It takes the church to uphold visions such as these. They wrote the vision down (Hab. 2:4), and others who help financially run after it. To starve them is to starve the vision of Christ.

Not all giving is in wisdom or of God. Neither is the spending of all donated church finances. One thing we know—the devil or the spirit of man will never cause anyone to give, spread the gospel, or encourage prayer. Those who uphold these ministries give because of the burden of the Lord placed on them. These still need to flow with a truly God given FIVE-FOLD MINISTRY STRUCTURE. They need to encourage and seek out God's direction in how to flow with and incorporate five-fold ministry principles.

Full Time Ministry

There are times when a ministry in full flight needs to attend to ministry full time. Many major ministries do so and would be wrong if they did not. This usually applies to some evangelist, teacher or prophet ministries, and a few pastors as well. This does not take away from the proper scriptural financial dealings within the churches. When one ministry takes a salary and ignores the other ministries and elders, they are lording over God's heritage. When this effectively limits the multiple ministry, as well as the ministry to the poor, something is wrong. If the apostle is not sought out to head up the work and is not upheld financially, the financial focus is out of order. The multiple eldership and ministry needs to function, and we need to seek God's wisdom and ways to allow this to be. Some major and well known church pastors, if they truly are that, are so busy they never keep up. May they seek out the other God provided ministries to flow and balance the work. This needs to be considered financially as well.

Luke 16:10, 11, and 12, "He who is faithful in what is least is faithful also in much; and he who is unjust in what is least is unjust also in much. Therefore if you have not been faithful in the unrighteous mammon , who will commit to your trust the true riches? And if you have not been faithful in what is another man's, who will give you what is your own?" May we yield all we are and ever could be to the Lord Jesus Christ. May his Kingdom come within us.

Deep down, some ministries are fine in the eyes of man, but are secretly disappointed in their walk and relationship with God. Perhaps God wants to give you much more, but is unable to since you have not been faithful in the natural mammon (money).

FIVE-FOLD FOUNDATION MINISTRY and a multiple eldership will not flow properly until we learn how to deal properly with church finances. Changing our habitual practices and dealing with this issue will take a willingness to change. May we be willing to pay the price. We are facing what Paul spoke of in 1 Timothy 6:10, "For the love of money is the root of all evil: which while some coveted after, they have erred from the faith." Since much evil is prevalent, there is a great love of money, and the selfish "I" comes to the fore here as in no other place.

A text we often hear, and the one most Christians are aware of, is found in the Old Testament. "Bring ye all the tithes into the storehouse, that there may be meat in mine house, and prove me now herewith, saith the LORD of hosts, if I will not open you the windows of heaven, and pour you out a blessing."

How true this text is! The finances should truly provide meat in God's storehouse, to provide for his purposes family and gospel, according to the full scriptural portrayal.

May we be faithful in giving, using the finances of God, and distributing them in the way that pleases Him. His blessing will surely follow if we do. Look for heaven's open windows. May we bow our knee at the throne of our Lord, the Alpha and Omega, our soon coming King of Kings and Lord of Lords. May we bow at His Word. That is the worship in truth Jesus spoke of. May we not only serve Him, but walk with Him, for now and for eternity.

If you love Jesus, may the Love, grace, comfort and mercy of our triune living God be with you.

Love in Christ,
Your Brother
John

P.S. Give my love to Marion and the children.

SUMMARY

We pray the prayer, "May thy Kingdom come on earth as it is in heaven." Jesus is Lord of heaven, and all heaven is totally yielded to His authority. When we pray this prayer in agreement with our Father God, we are saying we desire His authority be established on earth as well, and especially in the church.

May we take a serious look at what would happen if this prayer were answered. When this prayer is answered, the glory of the latter house will be greater than the glory of the former house (Hagg. 2:9). We will see a church much like the first century church and the New Testament example. May we not rest until we see all the New Testament portrays becomes a reality today. The same Holy Ghost promised to you and to your children and as many as are afar off, whom the Lord shall call, is here now (Acts 2:39). May we do our all to allow Him place and total control of all ministry within the church. May we begin by searching out every place where we differ from the example of the New Testament church.

The government of the church is a major subject, an important issue and doctrine. God's order in church government needs to be searched out diligently and followed. All scriptures are given to us for doctrine (2 Tim. 3:16). When we transgress by not applying scriptural truths, even though we are convinced of their content, we walk in darkness. Jesus said, "If the light that is in you become darkness, how great is that darkness."

Soon this whole world as we know it will be no more. Soon the night will be upon us when we can no longer work. Soon the last soul shall come in and then the judgment of God will follow. I want to hear the words "Well done, thou good and faithful servant." May we shun the accolades of men and empire vision, seeking only the approval of the Father of our Lord and Savior Jesus Christ. May we pay any price necessary to follow our Lord and His directives. May we love the unbeliever to Christ, knowing His will that none should perish. May we worship our

Lord in truth, and follow only His will and instructions as we build the church.

God's ministry and church structure must come into order. May we not pattern ourselves after the world. God's kingdom is not a democracy. It is an Imperial government under our God and King. Jesus Christ is the Lord of the church. May we allow Him His rightful place.

He gives a multiple ministry banquet table. He has set out His desire for His authority structure of His church government. We need to heed His directions. To deny His given multiple ministry is to deny His Lordship. Even if we see apparent success in our solo ministry, we need to remember that some will preach the gospel out of contention and still see results. May we desire our risen Lord's approval above all things. May we esteem our brothers better than ourselves, because Christ called them and gave them to us. May we humbly seek out and encourage all ministries and elders as well as the family of believers.

May we see world evangelism, the founding and structuring of the church, and establishing of the new believers, as the most important issues in our lives next to our personal salvation. The gospel will advance when apostles, prophets and teachers are given their rightful place within the church, along with the more accepted evangelists and pastors (Eph. 4:11, 1 Cor. 12:28).

May we worship our Lord and King with all that we have and are! May we not shrink from paying the price to establish His true Lordship at any level. May the cost of our personal power realm, image, financial welfare, and ego be humbled and laid at His feet. No idols. Only one God, who is worthy of our worship and praise. May thy Kingdom come, our Lord God and soon coming King, on earth as it is in heaven.

COPIES AVAILABLE FROM

FIVE-FOLD FOUNDATION MINISTRIES,
PUBLISHING DIVISION
P.O. BOX 205,
POST FALLS, IDAHO 83854
U.S.A.

1996 PRICE $10.95 U.S. (plus shipping)
Volume discounts available,
including special pricing for Bible schools, etc.

Book sales benefit foreign translations and ministry.